Register This New Book

Benefits of Registering*

- ✓ FREE **replacements** of lost or damaged books
- ✓ FREE **audiobook** – *Pilgrim's Progress*, audiobook edition
- ✓ FREE information about new titles and other **freebies**

www.anekopress.com/new-book-registration

*See our website for requirements and limitations.

Moody's LATEST SERMONS

UNWAVERING FAITH and COMMITMENT to CHRIST

D. L. Moody

We enjoy hearing from our readers. Please contact us at www.anekopress.com/questions-comments with any questions, comments, or suggestions.

Moody's Latest Sermons
© 2022 by Aneko Press
All rights reserved. First edition 1900.
Revisions copyright 2022.

Please do not reproduce, store this edition in a retrieval system, or transmit in any form or by any means – electronic, mechanical, photocopying, recording, or otherwise, without written permission from the publisher. Please contact us via www.AnekoPress.com for reprint and translation permissions.

Scripture quotations from The Authorized (King James) Version. Rights in the Authorized Version in the United Kingdom are vested in the Crown. Reproduced by permission of the Crown's patentee, Cambridge University Press.

Cover Designer: Jonathan Lewis

Aneko Press
www.anekopress.com
Aneko Press, Life Sentence Publishing, and our logos are trademarks of
Life Sentence Publishing, Inc.
203 E. Birch Street
P.O. Box 652
Abbotsford, WI 54405
RELIGION / Christian Living / Spiritual Growth
Paperback ISBN: 978-1-62245-904-9
eBook ISBN: 978-1-62245-905-6

10 9 8 7 6 5 4 3 2 1

Available where books are sold

Contents

Ch. 1: The Ninety-First Psalm 1

Ch. 2: The Eighth Chapter of Romans 17

Ch. 3: Temptation 43

Ch. 4: Four Questions from God 57

Ch. 5: The Transfiguration 69

Ch. 6: Mary and Martha 85

Ch. 7: A Need for Revival 109

Dwight L. Moody – A Brief Biography 131

Other Similar Titles 133

Chapter 1

The Ninety-First Psalm

This was the last address delivered by D. L. Moody on Round Top, where his body now lies awaiting the resurrection.

This psalm might have been written by Moses after some terrible calamity had come upon the children of Israel. It might have been after that terrible night of death in Egypt, when the first-born from the palace to the hovel were slain; or after that terrible plague of fiery serpents in the wilderness, when the people were full of fear and in a nervous state. In the Western states, where they have terrible cyclones, the people, old and young, get very nervous, and whenever they see a cloud coming up, they are alarmed. I was in Iowa some time ago, after they had had in that state seven cyclones, one right after another. They had been all around the city that I was in, and if a storm came up and the black clouds began to gather, the whole city was just trembling.

Perhaps Moses called Aaron and Miriam, and Joshua and Caleb, and a few others into his tent and read this psalm to them first. How sweet it must have sounded, and how strange!

I can imagine Moses asking, "Do you think that will help them? Will that quiet them?" and they all thought that it would. And then, (it may be), on one of those hill-tops of Sinai, at twilight, this psalm was read. How it must have soothed them, how it must have helped them, how it must have strengthened them!

You will notice in the last two verses there are seven things that God told Moses He would do, seven "I wills." If they could get burned down into our souls, it would be a help to us all through life. When God says He will do a thing, there is no power on earth or in perdition than can keep Him from doing that which He has promised to do.

I. "I Will Deliver"

First, "I will deliver." When God called Moses to go down into Egypt to deliver the children of Israel from the hand of the Egyptians, in all the world there wasn't a man who, humanly speaking, was less qualified than Moses. He had made the attempt once before to deliver the children of Israel, and he began by delivering one man. He failed in that, and killed an Egyptian, and had to run off into the desert, and stay there forty years. He had tried to deliver the Hebrews in his own way, he was working in his own strength and doing it in the energy of the flesh. He had all the wisdom of the Egyptians, but that didn't help him. He had to be taken back into Horeb, and kept there forty years in the school of God, before God could trust him to deliver the children of Israel in God's way. Then God came to him and said, "I have come down to deliver," and when God worked through Moses three million were delivered as easy as I can turn my hand over. God could do it. It was no trouble when God came on the scene.

Learn the lesson. If we want to be delivered, from every inward and outward foe, we must look to a higher source than ourselves. We cannot do it in our own strength.

We all have some weak point in our character. When we would go forward, it drags us back, and when we would rise up into higher spheres of usefulness and the atmosphere of heaven, something drags us down. Now I have no sympathy with the idea that God puts us behind the blood and saves us, and then leaves us in Egypt to be under the old taskmaster. I believe God brings us out of Egypt into the promised land, and that it is the privilege of every child of God to be delivered from every foe, from every besetting sin.

> It is the privilege of every child of God to be delivered from every foe, from every besetting sin.

If there is some sin that is getting the mastery over you, you certainly cannot be useful. You certainly cannot bring forth fruit to the honor and glory of God until you get self-control. "He that ruleth his spirit is better than he that taketh a city." If we haven't got victory over jealousy, over envy, over self-seeking and covetousness and worldly amusements and worldly pleasure, if we are not delivered from all these things, we are not going to have power with God or with men, and we are not going to be as useful as we might be if we got deliverance from every evil. There isn't an evil within or without but what He will deliver us from if we will let Him. That is what He wants to do. As God said to Moses, "I have come down to deliver." If He could deliver three million slaves from the hands of the mightiest monarch on earth, don't you think He can deliver us from every besetting sin, and give us complete victory over ourselves, over our temper, over our dispositions, over our irritableness and peevishness and snappishness? If we want it and desire it above everything else, we can get victory.

People are apt to think that these little things (as we call them) are weaknesses that we are not responsible for; that they are misfortunes, that we inherited them. I have heard people talk about their temper. They say,

"Well, I inherited it from my father and mother; they were quick-tempered, and I got it from them."

Well, that is a poor place to hide, my friend. Grace ought to deliver us from all those things.

A lady came to me some time ago and said she had great trouble with her temper now, and she was more irritable than she was five years ago, and she wanted to know if I didn't think it was wrong.

I said, "I should think you are backsliding. If you

haven't better control over yourself now than you had five years ago, there is something radically wrong."

"Well," she said, "I should like to know how I am going to mend it. Can you tell me?"

"Yes."

"How?"

I said, "When you get angry with people and give them a good scolding, go right to them after you have made up your mind that you have done wrong, and tell them you have sinned and ask them to forgive you."

She said she wouldn't like to do that.

Of course she wouldn't; but she will never get victory until she treats it as sin. Don't look upon it as weakness or misfortune, but SIN. No child of God ought to lose control of temper without confessing it.

A lady came to me some time ago and said that she had got so in the habit of exaggerating that people accused her of misrepresentation. She wanted to know if there was any way she could overcome it.

"Certainly," I said.

"How?"

"Next time you catch yourself at it, go right to the party and tell them you lied."

"Oh!" she said, "I wouldn't like to call it lying."

Of course not, but a lie is a lie all the same, and you will never overcome those sins until you treat them as sins and get them out of your nature. If you want to shine in the light of God and be useful, you must overcome, you must be delivered. And that is what God says He will do; He will deliver.

II. "I Will Answer"

Now, the next "I will" – "He shall call upon me, and I will answer him."

There is a chance for all of us to call. The great God that made heaven and earth has promised, "I will answer his call." If you call on God for deliverance and for victory over sin and every evil, God isn't going to turn a deaf ear to your call. I don't care how black your life has been, I don't care what your past record has been, I don't care how disobedient you have been, I don't care how you have back-slidden and wandered; if you really want to come back, God accepts the willing mind, God will hear your prayer, and answer.

Listen to the prodigal: "Father, I have sinned!" That was enough; the father took him right to his bosom. The past was blotted out at once. Look at the men on the day of Pentecost. Their hands were dripping with the blood of the Son of God; they had murdered Jesus Christ. And what did Peter say to them? "It shall come to pass, that whosoever shall call on the name of the Lord shall be saved." Look at the penitent thief. It might have been that when a little boy, his mother taught him that same passage in Joel, "It shall come to pass, that whosoever shall call on the name of the Lord shall be saved." As he hung there on the cross, it flashed into his mind that this was the Lord of glory, and though he was on the very borders of hell, he cried out, "Lord, remember me," and the answer came right then and there, "This day thou shalt be with Me in paradise." In the morning associated with thieves; in the evening, associated with the purest of heaven. In the morning, cursing – Matthew and Mark both tell us that those two thieves came out cursing; in the evening, uplifted on high, an inhabitant of heaven. In the morning, as black as hell could make him; in the evening, not a spot or wrinkle. Why? Because he took God at His word.

My dear friend, if you are unsaved, you just call upon God now, and here is a promise, "I will answer his call."

A few years ago an old returned missionary went to one of our leading hospitals to have a surgical operation performed. He was to go under ether, and it was doubtful whether he would come out or not; he might wake up in another world. He bade adieu to his friends, gave them his farewell blessing – he was a very godly man – and when the doctor said, "Well, we are ready," he faced them, and with a calm look, he said:

"Would you just wait a minute?"

Then he lifted his voice in prayer –

"Now I lay me down to sleep,
I pray the Lord my soul to keep.
If I should die before I wake,
I pray the Lord my soul to take."

Then, opening his eyes, he said, "Doctor, I am ready," and passed under the knife, and out from under it into health.

My dear friends, it is a sweet privilege to pray; it is a sweet privilege to be in touch with heaven, to be in communion with the great God that made heaven and earth. "I will answer his call."

I suppose there isn't a Christian in this audience but can say Amen to that. You can say God has answered in the past, and you believe He will do so again.

Some people say they can't call. Perhaps you cannot make an eloquent prayer – I hope you can't – I have heard about all the eloquent prayers I want to. But you can say, "God, be merciful to me, a sinner."

Only be sincere, and God will hear your cry. Mark you, there is a sham cry. Mothers understand that; they know when their children cry in earnest, or whether it is a sham cry. Let the child give a real cry of distress, and the mother will leave everything and fly to her child. I have been forty years in Christian work, and I have never known God to disappoint any man or woman who was in earnest about their soul's salvation. I know lots of people who pretend to be in earnest, but their prayers are never answered.

III. "I Will Be with Him in Trouble"

Every heart knows its own bitterness. If the troubles that are represented by this audience could be written in a volume, it would take the biggest volume you have ever seen. We are apt to think that young people do not have any trouble, but if they haven't, there is one thing they can make sure of, that they are going to have trouble later. "Man is born unto trouble, as the sparks fly upward." Trouble is coming. No one is exempt. God has had one Son without sin, but He has never had one without sorrow. Jesus Christ, our Master, suffered as few men ever suffered, and He died very young. Ours is a path of sorrow and suffering, and it is so sweet to hear the Master say:

"I will be with you in trouble."

Don't let any one think for a moment that you can get on without Him. You may say now, "I can get on; I am in good health and prosperity," but the hour is coming when you will need Him.

Many a Christian could bear witness to this point, that He has been with them in trouble, that in some dark hour when the billows seemed to be rolling up around them, they cried to Him, and He heard their cry, He answered their prayer, and He brought peace. There was joy in their sorrow, there was a star that lit up even the darkest night.

I remember being on that vessel, the *Spree*, when the shaft broke and a hole was knocked in her bottom out in mid-ocean, and the stern sank thirty feet. All my family but one was in Northfield, and I was making my way home, leaving friends in Europe. There I was in mid-ocean, pulled up, as it were, to look into my own grave for about forty-eight hours, without one ray of hope, humanly speaking. For forty-eight hours the burden was intense. My heart was like a lump of lead.

The accident happened Saturday morning. Sunday afternoon we had a prayer-meeting, and after prayer I read this ninety-first Psalm. If it had been let down from heaven, it could not have given more comfort. I went into my state room, and I fell on my knees, and I cried to the Lord:

"It is a time of trouble; help me."

And God took the burden. It rolled off, and I fell asleep. I never slept sounder than I did that night, and all the rest of the time. If a storm had burst on us any time during the week, we would have gone down, but God was with us in the time of trouble, and the burden was lifted.

A great many people seem to embalm their troubles. I always feel like running away when I see them coming. They bring out their old mummy, and tell you in a sad voice:

"You don't know the troubles I have!"

My friends, if you go to the Lord with your troubles, He will take them away. Would you not rather be with the Lord and get rid of your troubles, than be with your troubles and without God? Let trouble come if it will drive us nearer to God.

> Let trouble come if it will drive us nearer to God.

It is a great thing to have a place of resort in the time of trouble. How people get on without the God of the Bible is a mystery to me. If I didn't have such a refuge, a place to go and pour out my heart to God in such times, I don't know what I would do. It seems as if I would go out of my mind. But to think, when the heart is burdened, we can go and pour it into His ear, and then have the answer come back, "I will be with him," there is comfort in that!

I thank God for the old Book. I thank God for this old promise. It is as sweet and fresh to-day as it has ever been. Thank God, none of those promises are out of date, or grown stale. They are as fresh and vigorous and young and sweet as ever.

IV. "I Will Honor Him"

"I will honor him." God's honor is something worth seeking. Man's honor doesn't amount to much. Suppose Moses had stopped down there in Egypt. He would have been loaded down with Egyptian titles, but they would never have reached us. Suppose he had been Chief Marshal of the whole Egyptian army, "General" Moses, "Commander" Moses; suppose he had reached the throne and become one of those Pharaohs, and his mummy had come down to our day. What is that compared with the honor God put upon him?

"I will honor him." Didn't God put honor on Moses? How his name shines on the page of history! The honor of this world doesn't last; it is transient; it is passing away, and I don't believe any man or woman is fit for God's service that is looking for worldly preferment, worldly honors and worldly fame. Let us get it under our feet, let us rise above it, and seek the honor that comes down from above.

V. "With Long Life Will I Satisfy Him"

"With long life will I satisfy him." I get a good deal of comfort out of that promise. I don't think that means a short life down here, seventy years, eighty years, ninety years, or one hundred years. Do you think that any man living would be satisfied if they could live to be one hundred years old and then have to die? Not by a good deal. Suppose Adam had lived until to-day and had to die to-night, would he be satisfied? Not a bit of it! Not if he had lived a million years, and then had to die.

You know we are all the time coming to the end of things here – the end of the week, the end of the month, the end of the year, the end of school days. It is end, end, end all the time. But, thank God, He is going to satisfy us with long life; no end to it, an endless life.

Life is very sweet. I never liked death; I like life. It would be a pretty dark world if death was eternal, and when our loved ones die we are to be eternally separated from them. Thank God, it is not so; we shall be re-united. It is just moving out of this house into a better one; stepping up higher, and living on and on forever.

There is a verse – probably you have never noticed it – that came to me with great sweetness some time ago. It is in the 21st Psalm, the 4th verse: "He asked life of thee, and thou gavest it him, even length of days forever and ever." Think of that, length of days *forever and ever!*

Do you think Moses is dead yet?

He never lived as he does to-day, never; and he is going to live on and on forever. What does Christ say? "If a man keep My saying, he shall never taste of death." Never!

Don't you want to live forever? You can if you will. Eternal life is as free as the air that you and I take into our lungs. "Verily, verily, I say unto you, He that heareth

My word, and believeth on Him that sent Me, hath everlasting life, and shall not come into condemnation, but is passed from death unto life." Yes, "I will satisfy him with long life."

Is there any one here who hasn't got eternal life? I don't like to pass over this, and leave any one outside the kingdom. If you are not in, my friend, take my advice; don't eat, or drink, or sleep until you get eternal life. Then this body may be taken away, but if it is, you will make something out of death. "If our earthly house of this tabernacle is dissolved, we have a building of God, an house not made with hands, eternal in the heavens."

> Christ never preached a funeral sermon in the world. Death couldn't exist where He was.

When a young man, I was called upon suddenly, in Chicago, to preach a funeral sermon. A good many Chicago business men were to be there, and I said to myself,

"Now, it will be a good chance for me to preach the gospel to those men, and I will get one of Christ's funeral sermons."

I hunted all through the four Gospels trying to find one of Christ's funeral sermons, but I couldn't find any. I found He broke up every funeral He ever attended! He never preached a funeral sermon in the world. Death couldn't exist where He was. When the dead heard His voice they sprang to life. He will smash up the undertaking business when He comes to reign. "I am the resurrection and the life: he that believeth in Me, though he were dead, yet shall he live."

The 23d Psalm is more misquoted than anything else in the whole Bible. It is known in all the Catholic churches; it is known in the Greek church; it is in the Jewish synagogue; they chant it in a great many denominations, burying the dead; and armies went to battle chanting the 23d Psalm. And yet I believe it is more misquoted than anything in the Bible. People will weave it into their prayers, and conversation, and chapel services. They will say, "Yea, though I walk through the dark valley." They will always emphasize the word "dark," and send the cold chills running down your back. "Yea, though I walk through the *dark* valley of the shadow of death." I want to tell you, my dear friends, the word "dark" isn't there at all. The devil sticks that in there to confuse believers. It is, "Yea, though I walk through the valley of the shadow of death."

What is the difference?

Must not there be light where there is shadow? Can you get a shadow without light? If you doubt it, go down into the cellar to-night without a light, and find your shadow if you can. All that death can do to a true believer is to throw a shadow across his path. Shadows never hurt any one. You can walk right through shadows as you can through fog, and there is nothing to fear.

I pity down deep in my heart any man or woman that lives under the bondage of death! If you are under it, may God bring you out to-day! May you come right out into the liberty of the blessed gospel of the Son of God.

Jesus Christ came into the world to destroy death,

and we can say with Paul, if we will, "Oh death, where is thy sting?" and we can hear a voice rolling down from heaven saying, "Buried in the bosom of the Son of God." He took death unto His own bosom. He went into the grave to conquer and overthrow it, and when He arose from the dead said, "Because I live, ye shall live also." Thank God, we have a long life with Christ in glory.

My dear friends, if we are in Christ we are never going to die. Do you believe that? If sometime you should read that D. L. Moody, of East Northfield, is dead, don't believe a word of it. He has gone up higher, that is all; gone out of this old clay tenement into a house that is immortal, a body that death cannot touch, that sin cannot taint, a body fashioned like unto His own glorious body. Moses wouldn't have changed the body he had at the transfiguration for the body he had at Pisgah. Elijah wouldn't have changed the body he had at the transfiguration for the body he had under the juniper tree. They got better bodies; and I too am going to make something out of death.

VI. "I Will Set Him on High"

"I will set him on high." God is able to do it. Up above the angels, up above the archangels, up above the cherubims and seraphims, on the throne with His own Son.

We are called to be sons and daughters of the eternal God. Do you know, the Prince of Wales cannot sit on the throne with Queen Victoria; they wouldn't allow it. The heir to the throne of Russia has just recently died, and they have appointed another to take his place, but he cannot sit on the throne with his brother, the Czar.

But it is not so yonder. Christ has gone up and taken His seat at the right hand of the Father, and every son and daughter of God is to be lifted up onto the throne. My dear friends, think of the promise. Isn't it rich, isn't it sweet? "I will set him on high."

So that when our friends pass up to be on high and to be forever with Him, they are far better off.

VII. "I Will Show Him My Salvation"

"I will show him my salvation." That is a sweet promise. God can say to the angels – "Hark to that man that was once down in the depths, down in the gutter, but now he is lifted up and set upon my throne with my Son." Thank God for the riches of His grace in Christ Jesus!

I believe we don't learn the fringe of the subject of salvation down here. When our Master was on earth, He said He had many more things to say, but He could not reveal them to His disciples because they were not ready to receive them. But when we go yonder, where these mortal bodies have put on immortality, when our spiritual faculties are loosed from the thralldom of the flesh, I believe we shall be able to take more in. God will lead us from glory to glory, and show us the fullness of our salvation. Don't you think Moses knew more at the Mount of Transfiguration than he did at Pisgah? Didn't Christ talk with him then about the death He was to accomplish at Jerusalem? He couldn't have received this truth before, any more than the disciples, but when he had received his glorified body, Christ could show him everything.

Chapter 2

The Eighth Chapter of Romans*

This was the last formal address delivered by Mr. Moody in the Auditorium at Northfield.

The 8th chapter of Romans is one of the most famous chapters in all of Paul's epistles. I say, one of the most famous. There are three chapters that I think are highwater mark, and when I get into one of them I think that is the best, and when I get into the second one, I think that is the best, and when I get into the third, I think that is the best. I have three children; I think they are all the best. I can't tell which I like the best, but I like all three of them.

The 13th chapter of I Corinthians, that treatise on love, is sublime, and if the church of God could live in that chapter for twelve months, I believe it would revolutionize this country. I am quite sure the church of God itself would be revolutionized. Or the 15th chapter of I Corinthians, where Paul tells us what the gospel is, how Christ died for our sins and how He was raised for our justification, and where he teaches the mighty doctrine of the resurrection and the precious truth of His coming again; when I get there, I think that is about the best chapter. And then I turn to the 8th chapter of Romans, and when I get right into the heart of it, I really think that it is the best chapter Paul ever wrote.

This is the chapter that opens with no condemnation and closes with no separation. But mark you, it doesn't say there are no faults, no infirmities; it says there is no condemnation, either in life, or in death, or at the judgment. A great many people live all their lifetime under the bondage of death, and they fear the judgment; but if a man's life is hid with Christ in God, there is nothing to fear in time or in eternity. There is nothing that will give the believer so much comfort as to know his standing in Christ.

> For a man whose life is hid with Christ in God, judgment is already passed.

Note that the difference between a believer and an unbeliever is right here. An unbeliever is living in his day, and he has nothing but a long dark eternal night to look forward to; a Christian is now living in his night, and he has a grand morning that he is looking forward to. The day is ahead, the glory is ahead, the best of life is ahead; it is not behind. That is the teaching of

Scripture; and for a man whose life is hid with Christ in God, judgment is already passed; he will not come into judgment. Christ was judged for me, and the judgment is behind me, instead of before me. John 5:24: "Verily, verily, I say unto you, He that heareth my word, and believeth on him that sent me, hath everlasting life, and shall not come into condemnation; but is passed from death unto life." Already passed from death unto life.

Adoption, Sonship and Heirship

You will notice, as you pass along through this eighth chapter of Romans, how Paul brings out the thought of adoption, sonship and heirship. If I am adopted, I have become a child; God is no longer my judge, but my Father. It makes all the difference in the world how we look upon God. Some people fear God, but when they understand that He is their Father, that fear is gone.

Look a moment at the fourth verse: "That the righteousness of the law might be fulfilled in us, who walk not after the flesh, but after the Spirit." If we have been born of the Spirit, and have the divine life within us, we are not to follow after the flesh, but after the Spirit. Do you know that the flesh and the Spirit divide all men, and there is no third state? Either we are in the flesh and following after the flesh, or we are in the Spirit and following after the Spirit.

Note the fourfold description: first, their nature, after the flesh; second, they mind the things of the flesh; third, their state is death, dead to spiritual things; fourth, carnal-minded and cannot please God.

The flesh has its religion. You will find hardly a man to-day on the face of the earth that hasn't some sort of religion. You will find people living in the blackest, vilest kinds of sin, and you begin to talk with them, and they tell you:

"I won't give up my religion for yours."

That woman that Christ met at the well of Sychar was looking for the Messiah; she was a disciple of Jacob; she was all right. Yet she was living in the vilest kind of sin. We find the same state of things now. What is your creed good for if it hasn't got grace in it, and if there is no regeneration? A man told me the other day that he wanted a religion that was beautiful. There are a good many of that kind now; they want a dead cold formalism; they don't want anything that has life in it. A man got quite angry some time ago because I said religion had something to do with his moral character. He had divorced the two. That is human; that is man's religion.

Now, people say, "Well, how can you tell?"

Paul, in his letter to the Galatians, has drawn the picture so vividly that no one need be deceived. Let me read to you a few words from the 5th chapter of Galatians, the 19th verse: "Now the works of the flesh are manifest, which are these; adultery, fornication, uncleanness, lasciviousness, idolatry, witchcraft, hatred, variance, emulations, wrath, strife, seditions, heresies, envyings, murders, drunkenness, revellings, and such like: of the which I tell you before, as I have also told you in time past, that they which do such things shall not inherit the kingdom of God."

People have an idea now that it makes very little

difference what a man believes if he is only sincere, if he is only honest in his creed. I believe that is one of the greatest lies that ever came out of the pit of hell. Why, they virtually say you can believe a lie just as well as you can believe the truth, if you are only in earnest, and stick to it.

Suppose I go to a bank and present a check for $10,000, and the cashier says:

"Have you any money in this bank?"

I say, "No, nor in any other bank."

"What are you drawing this check on?"

"Earnestness. There isn't a man in Massachusetts who wants to get $10,000 as much as D. L. Moody."

They would have me in a madhouse inside of thirty days, if not inside of thirty hours; and you people who say it doesn't make any difference what a man believes, you are deluded by Satan!

The time has come when a line should be drawn between the church and the world, and every Christian should get both feet out of the world. The trouble to-day is with these border Christians – that are living on the border, and that constantly want to slip over into Egypt, and get some of the onions and leeks and garlic. The most miserable people I meet are these border Christians. They are trying to live for both worlds, and are off and on, and you never know where to find them.

> The most miserable people I meet are these border Christians. They are trying to live for both worlds.

When the civil war was going on, the border states suffered more than any other part of the country. The states that were farther south, where they didn't have any fighting, didn't suffer like Kentucky and Maryland and Virginia. Every inch of that ground was fought over. In some places there were people who tried to be on both sides. They had the Confederate flag and the Star Spangled Banner, and when the Union army came along they ran up the American flag and shouted themselves hoarse for the Union, and when they passed, and the Confederate army came along, they put up the Confederate flag. Do you know what happened? Both armies had utter contempt for them, and they burned down their houses to the ground.

Next Paul goes on to tell what the fruit of Spirit is. "The fruit of the Spirit is love, joy, peace, long-suffering, gentleness, goodness, faith, meekness, temperance; against such there is no law. And they that are Christ's have crucified the flesh with the affections and lusts. If we live in the Spirit, let us also walk in the Spirit. Let us not be desirous of vain-glory, provoking one another, envying one another."

Isn't it put clear there? Haven't you there the fruits of the flesh, and the fruit of the Spirit? It seems to me no man or woman need be in doubt as to where they stand, which side they are on. What kind of fruit are you bringing forth?

Now, the best part of the natural man is his mind, isn't it? Let the mind move out of this body, and I am shut up in some institution. Now, Paul teaches that the carnal mind is enmity against God (verse 7). If the best part of a man is enmity against God, and isn't subject to the law of God, as, indeed, it cannot be, according to the Scripture, then we must put off the flesh, must we not, and not try to serve God in the flesh? "For to be carnally-minded is death; but to be spiritually-minded is life and peace; because the carnal mind is enmity against God; for it is not subject to the law of God, neither, indeed, can be."

I have had mothers come to me and say, "Mr. Moody, don't you think it is strange that my boy doesn't like spiritual things?"

I always say, "No; it would be a very strange thing if he did, until he is born of the Spirit."

The carnal mind likes carnal things, the natural mind likes natural things, the worldly mind likes worldly things; but the spiritually-minded man likes spiritual things. The man that has become a partaker of the divine nature wants food for that nature, food that comes from heaven. This world will never satisfy him. He has a nature that reaches out after God. "Old things are passed away; behold, all things are become new." He doesn't have to give up the world; the world slips away from him; he has something better. But the carnal man, of course, he likes the world; why shouldn't he?

Now there are three stumbling-stones in the way of every man – human religion, human wisdom and human righteousness. In a great many of our colleges they are leaving this old Book out entirely, and they are trying to get wisdom without the Word of God and without the mind of God and without any knowledge of God. Daniel tells us that men shall run to and fro, and knowledge shall be increased. I believe that day has come. There never has been a day when knowledge has been sweeping over the earth as it is at the present time.

We are living in a most marvelous age. A boy sixteen years old knows more than his father did one hundred years ago at the age of fifty. He has more advantages. But this doesn't mean that righteousness is increasing. Therefore, let us be wary.

If it never troubles a man's conscience to spend a great deal of his time in questionable places of amusement, and to take his family into places where there are degraded people, if he drives like Jehu all the week to make a dollar and moves like a snail on the Sabbath toward spiritual things – I believe that man is following the flesh; the divine nature is not in him; he is not walking after the Spirit, but after the flesh. When I find Christian people who had rather go to some progressive euchre party or whist party than to a religious meeting, I think they are following the flesh, don't you? I was perfectly shocked when at Pittsburg some time ago to find that some church members left the town Sunday night and went to Philadelphia to attend a whist association. Is it any wonder their children go to ruin? Oh, God hates a sham! It means a good deal to be a Christian, and if a person is going to be a Christian, let him put off the old man with all his deeds and put on the new man. That is the kind of Christians we need at the present time, "for to be carnally-minded is death; but to be spiritually-minded is life and peace."

What are we going to do with the flesh? Let it be abolished! Let it be destroyed! Let us put it in the place of death, and keep it there. It is not God's plan to bring this corrupt body into His kingdom; it is going to be cast off at death, and, therefore, we had better put it away now.

Look at that ninth verse: "But ye are not in the flesh, but in the Spirit, if so be that the Spirit of God dwell in you. Now if any man have not the Spirit of Christ, he is none of His."

How are you going to tell whether you are a Christian or not? Not by the fact that you are a Catholic or a Protestant, not that you subscribe to some creed that man has drawn up. We must have something better than that. What did Christ say? "By this shall all men know that you are My disciples, if you have love one for another." I used to wish, when I was first converted, that every Christian had to wear a badge, because I would like to know them; my heart went out toward the household of faith. But I have got over that. Every hypocrite would have a badge on inside of thirty days, if Christianity had become popular. No badge outside; but God gives us a badge in the heart. The man that hasn't any love in his religion, I don't want it; it is human. The man that hasn't any love in his creed may let it go to the winds; I don't want it. "By this shall all men know that ye are my disciples, that you have love one toward another." That is the fruit of the Spirit. "If any man hath not the Spirit of Christ, he is none of His."

The Love of God

The quicker every church that hasn't the love of God is swept from the face of the earth, the better. They are stumbling-stones. They do far more harm than good. Our churches would not be empty, and our church members off on their bicycles on the Sabbath, or reading the Sunday newspapers, if the church of God was filled with love. Nothing will take hold of the hearts of people like love. If I can convince a man that I love him, it will break down every barrier, and I can reach him; there is a time coming in his life when I can reach him if I only bide my time, if I am filled with love.

You know the old story of the boy and the echo. The boy, living on the edge of the woods, heard the echo of his voice, and he cried out,

"Halloa there!"

The answer came, "Halloa there!"

"You are a bad boy!"

"You are a bad boy!"

"Come here, and I'll whip you!"

"Come here, and I'll whip you!"

"I am coming!"

"I am coming!"

The little fellow ran into the house and said, "Mother, there is a bad boy out in the woods, and he is going to whip me."

The mother said, "No, I don't think he is a bad boy; you didn't talk to him well. If you had spoken to him kindly I think he would have spoken to you kindly. Go out and try it again."

So the boy went out.

"Halloa!"

"Halloa!"

"You are a good boy!"

"You are a good boy!"

"I love you!"

"I love you!"

He came running into the house, and said, "Mother, that is a good boy, after all."

Life is only an echo. If you go through the world with love in your heart, you will make people love you; and love is the badge that Christ gave his disciples.

In the 10th, 11th, and 13th verses there are four "Ifs" that I want to call your attention to. "*If* Christ be in you, the body is dead because of sin; but the Spirit is life because of righteousness." "*If* the Spirit of Him that raised up Jesus from the dead dwell in you, He that raised up Christ from the dead shall also quicken your mortal bodies by His Spirit that dwelleth in you." "*If* ye live after the flesh, ye shall die." "*If* ye through the Spirit do mortify the deeds of the body, ye shall live." Mark it. We are to walk by the Spirit, we are to be led by the Spirit, we are to be taught by the Spirit, we are to be influenced by the Spirit, we are to be guided by the Spirit, we are to be inhabited by the Spirit; and if these bodies become a temple for the Holy Ghost to dwell in, and we put off the old man with all his deeds, and put on the new man, then we shall have power with God and man, we shall get victory over sin, over the world, and over Satan – over every foe. But it is *in* Christ.

But look again, in the 15th verse: "For ye have not received the spirit of bondage again to fear; but ye have received the Spirit of adoption, whereby we cry, Abba, Father."

I want to say very emphatically that I have no sympathy with the doctrine of universal brotherhood, and universal fatherhood; I don't believe one word of it. If a man lives in the flesh and serves the flesh, he is a child of the devil. That is pretty strong language, but it is what Christ said. It brought down a hornet's nest on His head, and helped to hasten Him to the cross, but nevertheless it is true. Show me a man that will lie and steal and get drunk and ruin a woman – do you tell me he is my brother? Not a bit of it. He must be born into the household of faith before he becomes my brother in Christ. He is an alien, he is a stranger to the grace of God, he is an enemy to God, he is not a friend. Before a man can cry, "Abba, Father," he must be born from above, born of the Spirit.

"The Spirit Himself beareth witness with our spirit, that we are the children of God." Paul is climbing along up to this beautiful doctrine of sonship, but he is coming a different way from what the world does. "And if children, then heirs; heirs of God, and joint-heirs with Christ, if so be that we suffer with Him, that we may be also glorified together."

Oh, that we might know our true relationship! Sons and daughters of God in this crooked and perverse generation! Do you know that a great many children of God have never seen their standing in Christ, and what it means to be a son or a daughter?

They never rise above servants.

Go into a strange family, and see how long it takes you to find out who are the servants, and who the guests, and who the sons. I have been into many a home when I have been a stranger in a strange city; arrived late Saturday night; got up Sunday morning early, before any one was up except the servant. The servant would come in, and dust the room, and put the furniture in order; I knew that was the servant.

By and by a guest would come down, and I wouldn't be there five minutes before I would find that he was in the same position as myself. By and by down would come a rollicking boy, and away he would go all through the house, out into the kitchen, into one room after another; and if it was a week day, and the post had come, he would look over all the letters to see if there was a letter for him. You could tell the difference between a servant and a guest and a son.

What ailed that prodigal? Why, he was coming to say to his father, "Let me go into the kitchen and live with the servants. Make me as one of thy hired servants."

His father wouldn't hear a word of it. "Bring forth the best robe, and put it on him; and put a ring on his hand, and shoes on his feet: and bring hither the fatted calf, and kill it; and let us eat, and be merry: for this my son was dead, and is alive again." He called him his *son*, not *servant*.

My dear friends, we are sons; and if sons, we are heirs; and thank God, if we are heirs, we are joint-heirs with Jesus Christ.

What He is, so am I.

After the Chicago fire I met a man who said,

"Moody, I hear you lost everything in the Chicago fire."

"Well," I said, "you understood it wrong; I didn't."

He said, "How much have you left?"

"I can't tell you; I have got a good deal more left than I lost."

"You can't tell how much you have?"

"No."

"I didn't know you were ever that rich."

"I suppose you didn't."

"What do you mean?"

"I mean just what I say. I got my old Bible out of the fire; that is about the only thing. I saved it from the burning of that city, and one promise came to me that illuminated that city a good deal more than the fire did. 'He that overcometh shall inherit all things, and I will be his God.'"

You ask me how much I am worth. I don't know. You may go and find out how much the Vanderbilts are worth, and the Astors, and Rothschilds, but you can't find out how much a child of God is worth. Why? Because he is a joint-heir with Jesus Christ.

Why are you going around with your head down, talking about your poverty? The weakest, poorest child of God is richer than a Vanderbilt, because he has eternal riches. The stuff that burned up in Chicago was like the dust in the balance. Joint-heir with Jesus Christ! That is what the 8th of Romans teaches us.

Did you ever notice when Christ reached resurrection ground, what He said? "I ascend unto My Father,

THE EIGHTH CHAPTER OF ROMANS*

and your Father; and to My God and your God." He took us right into fellowship. Isn't that sweet?

Did you ever think that when Christ was dying on the cross, He made a will? Perhaps you have thought that no one ever remembered you in a will. You have been remembered, if you are in the kingdom. Christ remembered you in His will. He willed His body to Joseph of Arimathea, He willed His mother to John, the son of Zebedee – and what a legacy it was! better than bonds and stocks – and He willed his Spirit back to His Father. But to His disciples He said, "My peace, I leave that with you; that is my legacy. My joy, I give that to you." "My joy," think of it! "My peace give I unto you" – not *our* peace, but *His* peace!

> If Christ had left us gold, thieves would have stolen it; but He left His peace and His joy for every true believer.

They say a man can't make a will now that lawyers can't break, and drive a four-in-hand right straight through it. I will challenge them to break Christ's will; let them try it. No judge or jury can set that aside. Christ rose to execute His own will. If He had left us a lot of gold, thieves would have stolen it in the first century; we never would have got it; but He left His peace and His joy for every true believer. Get into the 8th chapter of Romans! Paul was down in the 7th; but he was up in the 8th chapter. He had both feet on the rock in the 8th. What a grand chapter it is!

Stop a moment, and ask yourself this question: Am I an heir, really an heir, of God? Are all these things mine? What does He say? "I appoint unto you a kingdom as My Father hath appointed" – that is joint-heirship, isn't it? – "that you might eat and drink with Me in My kingdom, and that you might sit with Me on My throne." Think of the Lord stooping down and taking a poor drunkard right up out of the gutter, and putting his feet on the rock, and a new song in his mouth, and lifting him up above powers and principalities, above angels and archangels, seraphims and cherubims, up, up, up, onto the throne with Himself! Do you suppose that an angel flying over the nations of the earth would look at any throne? What a great time they had a few years ago putting the Czar onto the throne of Russia! Nation after nation sent representatives to help lift him up. But Christ's is more than that. His is an everlasting kingdom. His is a throne that is going to endure forever; and He says, "Ye shall sit with Me on My throne." Man, look up! Look at the stars to-night! no mud to-night! Our inheritance is above.

How sweetly He utters these words: "In My Father's house." How tender! The same Spirit, the same place that He is in, the same hope, the same Grace, the same glory, and the same home!

This life is perfectly safe. Suppose that some one should lay hands upon the heir to the throne of England – every man in the English army and ever vessel in the navy would be brought out at once to defend him, if necessary. God will take care of the heirs of glory. How are they guarded? "The angels of God encamp round about them." Do you remember when that servant of Elisha got scared, Elisha said, "Lord, open his eyes," and he saw the mountains filled with horses and chariots of fire. Look up, and thank God for this promise!

I had rather be in the heart of the 8th of Romans than Adam in the heart of Paradise. Adam might have stayed in Paradise ten thousand years, and the devil could have come in then and snatched his life away from him, but I challenge the devil himself to get my life away from me, because it is hid with Christ in God, and Christ conquered Satan. "The prince of this world cometh, and hath nothing in Me." Christ conquered him, and oh, how safe the believer is! When the sinner is hid in Christ, hid in God, how is Satan going to get at him? He must go by the Almighty and by Christ before he can get at that sinner.

It is a great thing to be an heir of glory. It is a great thing to have your life guarded by the Son of God, and to have the angels of God encamping round about you.

"What shall we then say to these things? If God be for us, who can be against us?" (verse 31.) Would you just answer that question? Who can be against us if God, the Creator of heaven and earth, be for us? Why, no one!

Take the 28th verse: "And we know that all things work together for good to them that love God, to them that are called according to his purpose." All things: tribulation, reproaches, persecution, infirmities, distresses, famines, etc.; all things work together for good to them that love Him.

Do you know, a dead level in a man's life would be his ruin? If he had nothing but prosperity, he would be ruined. A man can stand adversity better than prosperity. I know a great many men who have become very prosperous, but I know few that haven't lost all their piety, that haven't lost sight of that city eternal in the heavens, whose builder and maker is God. Earthly things have drawn their heart's affections away from eternal things.

What we sigh and long for is very often the very ruin of us. Joseph was like most of us. He thought it was a pretty hard thing to be sold by his brothers, and taken off down into Egypt. It looked as if it was going to work against him. But didn't God overrule, and send him down there to lay by for all the nations of the earth? That star that began to shine down there has been shining ever since.

I have an idea we will thank God in eternity for our reverses and trials more than for anything else. I believe John Bunyan thanked God for the Bedford Jail more than for anything that happened to him down here. I believe Paul thanked God for the rods and stripes more than for anything else that happened to him; and he is talking right out of his own experience in this 8th of Romans. I haven't any doubt but that Daniel thought it was pretty hard to be taken as a captive, before he was twenty years old, off down into Babylon; but God sent him down there to tell the people how to live, and to light up that whole country. Not only that, he has been shining these twenty-five hundred years. What a record he has left behind him, to prove that all things "work together for good to them that love God," – the lion's den included. Little did he know, when he was cast into the lion's den, what a blessing he was going to be to the nations of the earth! Those young men didn't know what they were doing when they went into the fiery furnace, but what a blessing their experience has been to the church of God!

Man, are you passing through the waters? Don't get discouraged! You are an heir of glory, and if God calls you to pass through deep waters, go on; He is with you. He was with Joseph when he was cast into prison; they had to put the Almighty in with him. I had rather be in prison with the Almighty than outside without Him. You needn't be afraid of prison, and, my dear friends, you needn't be afraid of the grave, you needn't be afraid of death. Cheer up, child of God; the time of our redemption draweth near! We may have to suffer a little while, but when you think of the eternal weight of glory, you can afford to suffer, can't you?

I think we will be so ashamed of ourselves when we get to heaven, to remember we ever spoke about our sufferings. Christ said once that they that left everything for Him He would reward, and Peter asked:

"What are you going to give me?"

What had he left to follow Christ? A few old broken nets and fishing smacks.

I believe Peter was ashamed of that question a good many times afterward, when he got a taste of resurrection life and the glory beyond.

What have we left? I am tired and sick of people who are all the time talking about what they have to give up. Let that kind of talk go to the winds, and look and see what you have gained.

What Paul Knew

Here is one of Paul's favorite expressions, "*We know* that all things work together for good." I like to put down what John and Paul said about things they knew.

"*We know* whom we have believed." That is a good thing to know, isn't it?

"*We know* that we are of God." Why? "His Spirit bears witness with our spirit."

"*We know* that the Son of God hath come."

Oh, I am so tried of Christianity that is made up of negations, what people *don't* believe. I met a man some time ago, and he said, "I don't believe this." I talked with him a little, and made another statement; he didn't believe that. Finally, I said, "Man, will you tell me what you do believe?" and he didn't believe anything except that he didn't believe.

"*We know* we have passed from death unto life." Man, do *you* know it? If you don't, don't leave this hall to-night until you are sure you have passed from death unto life.

"*We know* that He abideth with us." Isn't that a great thing to know? If I have Christ formed in me the hope of glory, I can conquer this world and get it under my feet through Him; no other way.

"*We know* that He hears us." It is a good thing to live within speaking distance of heaven, and to get your prayers answered. You might as well tell me that I don't exist as to tell me God doesn't answer prayer. I would never stop to discuss that with a man, because God answers prayer every day.

THE EIGHTH CHAPTER OF ROMANS*

"*We know* that we shall appear with Him in glory. When Christ, who is our life, shall appear, then shall ye also appear with Him in glory." Cheer up, O child of God; the glory is ahead, not behind us.

"*We know* that when he shall appear, we shall be like Him." You say we are not like Him; we know it, but we shall be. That is something that is ahead. We shall be like Him, for we shall see Him as He is.

"*We know* that if our earthly house were dissolved, we have a building of God, an house not made with hands, eternal in the heavens." My dear friends, I am going to make something out of death. You talk about death being an enemy. It is the gateway to immortality. We pass through it to a glorious resurrection. I lay this body down, and I get a body even like His own glorious body, a body that death cannot touch, a body that sin cannot taint, a body like His own. Think of it!

I was down in Texas some time ago, and I happened to pick up a newspaper, and there they called me "Old Moody." Honestly, I never got such a shock from any paper in my life before! I never had been called old before. I went to my hotel, and looked in the looking glass.

My dear friends, I never felt so young in my life as I do to-night; I cannot conceive of getting old. I believe that I have a life that is never going to end. Death may change my position but not my condition, not my standing with Jesus Christ. Death is not going to separate us. That is the teaching of the 8th of Romans.

Old! I wish you all felt as young as I do here tonight. Why, I am only sixty-two years old! If you meet me ten million years hence, then I will be young. Read that 91st Psalm, "With long life will I satisfy him." That doesn't mean seventy years. Would that satisfy you? Did you ever see a man or woman of seventy satisfied? Don't they want to live longer? You know that seventy wouldn't satisfy you. Would eighty? would ninety? would one hundred? What will satisfy you? Ah, my friends, if Adam had lived to be a million years old, and had to die, he wouldn't be satisfied. "With long life will I satisfy him" – life without end. Don't call me old. I am only sixty-two. I am not old by a good deal.

Some Questions

Now Paul puts some questions. "Who can be against us? He that spared not His own Son, but delivered Him up for us all, how shall He not with Him also give us freely all things? (verse 32)." When God the Father gave Christ, the Son of His bosom, He literally gave up all that heaven had. He gave the richest jewel that heaven possessed. And if He has given us His Son, is there anything too great for us to ask? If a man should give me a diamond worth one hundred thousand dollars, I think I would make bold to ask him for a little piece of brown paper to carry it away in. If the Lord has given me the Son of His bosom, I can ask for anything. How shall He not freely give us all things?

He gave us His Son without anybody asking Him. No one dared to ask such a thing; He gave Him up freely for us all, says Paul. Thank God for the gift!

"Who shall lay anything to the charge of God's elect?" (verse 33). That is another question. Who will do it? How are you going to do it? "God that justifieth?" It would be a strange thing if God justified me, and then brought a charge against me.

That word "justifieth" seems too good to be true. No wonder that Martin Luther shook all Germany when that truth dawned upon him, "the just shall live by faith." Do you know what "justified" means? I will tell you. It is to stand before God without spot or wrinkle, without a sin. It is to be put back beyond Eden. God looks over His ledger, and says,

"Moody, I have no account against you; it has all been wiped out by another."

There is no condemnation. "Who is he that condemneth? Christ that died?"

Who will condemn me? Will Christ? Ten thousand times no! He wouldn't do it. That sweet verse, John 3:17, that has been overlooked. The 16th verse is so sublime that we forget the other. It is this: "For God sent not His Son into the world to condemn the world; but that the world through Him might be saved." Thank God, Christ didn't come to condemn, He came to save me. He left the bosom of the Father, stooped from yonder throne, and came down to this world that He might get His arm under the vilest sinner and lift him up to glory.

Haven't you sinned? I have. But if God has forgiven me, that is the end of it. What does the Bible say? "Not one of your sins shall be remembered." If God has put them away, they are gone for time and eternity. Oh, my friends, it is a great thing to be forgiven.

The next question is: "Who shall separate us from the love of Christ?" (verse 35).

Now, who is going to do it? Devils? men? angels? Paul throws down a challenge. He challenges heaven, and earth, and angels, and men, and principalities and powers; and not only that, but all things past, present and to come; all creatures internal or external; all states, death or life, height or preferment, depth or dungeon, prison or stripes – nothing shall separate me. Let the enemies come collectively or singly, I don't care. Let them come one and all. I have no foes that can overcome me. Why? Because God has justified me. I do not dread death; why? Because Christ has tasted death for me. I dread no judgment; why? That is past. I dread no separation, and I anticipate no failure.

If any man ever took a flight on earth, Paul did in closing up that eighth chapter of Romans. As some one has said, he rode triumphant in his chariot through heaven and earth, and he threw down the gauntlet and defied the enemies of God to come on. "Who shall separate us from the love of Christ? Shall tribulation, or distress, or famine or nakedness, or peril, or sword? For I am persuaded that neither death, nor life, nor angels, nor principalities, nor powers, nor things present, nor things to come, nor height, nor depth, nor any other creature, shall be able to separate us from the love of God which is in Christ Jesus our Lord." Nothing can separate us from the love of God, if we will just let the love of God into our hearts, and abide in His love.

There are three triplets in this chapter that I want to call your attention to:

The Trinity – God the Father, Christ the Son, and God the Holy Spirit.

Three "all things"; all things work together for good; all things He will freely give us; in all things we are more than conquerors.

Three groans – the groan of creation, the groan of the believer, the groan of the Holy Spirit. But in Revelation 5:13, the groans of creation cease. Thank God for that! Joseph Parker of London uttered something that I thought was splendid in regard to the 35th of Isaiah, where it says: "Sorrow and sighing shall flee away." Take up an old dictionary, he said, and once in a while you will come across a word marked "obsolete." The time is coming, he said, when those two words, "sorrow" and "sighing," shall be obsolete. Sighing and sorrow shall flee away, to be no more. Thank God for the outlook!

> Nothing can separate us from the love of God, if we will let the love of God into our hearts.

I thank God for the 8th chapter of Romans; and if you are not yet in it, get in and live there. It is a good place to live.

Chapter 3

Temptation

One of the most real things in this world is temptation, and the quicker we find it out the better.

When Christ was in the garden of Gethsemane praying, and His disciples were asleep, He woke them up, and said to them:

"Watch ye, and pray, lest ye enter into temptation. The spirit truly is ready, but the flesh is weak."

The flesh is weak. Is there any one on earth that dares to dispute that statement? Is there anything weaker under the sun than the human flesh? The spirit is willing. Most men would rather do the right thing, and think they will do it. Tell them that they will do certain things inside of twelve months, and they would say, as the king did, "Is thy servant a dog that he should do such a thing? No, never." But they will do it, just the same. "The spirit is willing, but the flesh is weak."

I don't suppose that one of those eleven men who gathered around Christ that night believed it. He spoke these words to the three that were in the inner circle – Peter, James, and John. No doubt they thought, "There is no danger of our falling. We can sleep all right, even when He tells us to be awake, and on the alert, and watching." But one of the twelve had already fallen, though they didn't know it. Peter, the chief speaker of the twelve, was going that very night to curse and swear, and say that he never knew Him. John and James were to leave Him, for "all forsook Him and fled." You probably couldn't find eleven better men on the face of the earth than those eleven; and yet Christ warned them that the spirit was willing, but the flesh was weak.

There has never been a man that has trod this earth that has not fallen some time in his life, except the Man Christ Jesus.

There is no one beyond the reach of the tempter. Keep that in mind. Life may run smoothly for a while, but the testing time is coming. Those eleven men were to be tempted that night as never before, and when the testing time came every one of them fell. "Watch and pray, lest ye enter into temptation; for the spirit is willing, but the flesh is weak." Oh, that God may open our eyes to see how very weak the flesh is! I believe firmly that if the iron plough has not gone down deep into a man's conscience, if he has not made a thorough work of sin, when the testing time comes, he will surely stumble and fall.

See what Christ says in the memorable parable of the Sower, found in Luke 8: "They on the rock are they, which, when they hear, receive the word with joy; and these have no root" – (a house on a rock is a very good thing, but it's a poor place for a tree) – "these have no root, which for a while believe, and in time of temptation fall away." Don't you see that in every-day life? Don't you know young men who started out and ran well for a season? Where are they to-day? What has become of them? They fell in the hour of temptation.

The strength of a chain is in its weakest link. Mark that; in its weakest link. Let a man be at work on the ceiling, and the platform be held up there with a chain of ten links, and one of the ten very weak. The testing time comes. The man steps on the platform. That one link gives way, and down comes the man just as surely as if every link breaks. So, bear in mind, fair-weather Christians are not going to stand the test; when the storms of temptation sweep over them, they will fall.

There is no dress parade about Christianity. When the battle comes, where are these fellows you see at dress parade? They are gone. And just so with a Christian that has to be bolstered up by a godly mother, or father, or friend, or it may be his wife. When they are gone, he is gone. I have seen it over and over again. Lot stood all right as long as he was with Abraham. When he left the plains of Mamre and went down into Sodom, away from Abraham, he stumbled and fell. I can find about one million Lots where you will find one Abraham today. Few men can stand alone when the storm sweeps over them. Away they go!

Have you ever been in a forest after a great storm has swept through it? Where the roots just run along on the surface and do not have any depth of earth, acres and acres of trees will be torn up. A friend from Scotland said to me, speaking of a place where I had been, "Some time ago they had a storm that blew down between four and five thousand of the finest trees on that old estate. Do you know why? Because the storm came in an unexpected direction. It had never come from that quarter before. It had blown in every direction but that one, and the forest wasn't prepared, and away the trees went."

It is said that Edinburgh Castle, in all the wars of Scotland, was never taken but once. Then the enemy came up the steep rocks at a place where the garrison thought it was so safe they needn't guard it. Very often temptation comes in an unexpected form or from an unexpected quarter, when you are off your guard; hence, the necessity of watching and praying, because if you are not on the alert, you will be tripped up by the tempter.

Then Christ adds: "Let him that thinketh he standeth, take heed lest he fall." No man on earth is beyond the reach of the tempter. I used to think that when I got along a certain distance in my Christian life I would get beyond the tempter, and he would have no more influence over me. I have given that up. The tempter will follow you from the cradle to the grave, and the nearer you get to Christ, the hotter the fight will be. As some one has said, Satan aims high. When he wanted one to sell the Lord, he went to the treasurer of the company; and when he wanted one to deny Him, he went to the chief apostle. When he wanted to call down fire from heaven on those Samaritans who refused the disciples hospitality, he went to John, who was nearest the heart of the Son of God. The angels fell, even in heaven. Adam fell in Paradise. Think of it!

Speaking of the four watches, some one has said, that the time a man is most liable to fall is in the second and the third watch. The first watch, he starts out, and says, "I must be on my guard; I am weak." He realizes his weakness, and keeps his eye upon the Master, going to Him daily and hourly for strength; and so he is not so liable to fall. But in the second and third watches he begins to feel his manhood, and says, "I am strong now, and I can stand." So he begins to lean on the arm of flesh, and then the peril comes, and the fall. As he gets into the fourth watch, he is nearing home, and he begins to see this old world receding from his vision. He realizes how weak the flesh is, because it has failed him so often, and he is on his guard again. He is not so liable to fall if he passes through the second and third watches, though he is always liable.

> The temptations that come to you and me are common to man.

Another thing about temptation. We are apt to think we have peculiar temptations. Not a bit of it; they are known to all men. See what Paul wrote to that church in Corinth:

"There hath no temptation taken you but such as is common to man: but God is faithful, who will not suffer you to be tempted above that ye are able; but will with the temptation also make a way to escape, that ye may be able to bear it."

Keep that in mind. The temptations that come to you and me are common to man. Every man who has gone on before us has had the same kind of temptation, although it may come to us in a different way. Men have always had the same jealousy to contend with, the same pride, and covetousness, and love of money, and love of pleasure, that you and I have.

There are four great temptations that threaten us to-day.

The Theatre

1. The theatre.

You say, "My folks go."

That may be. They may do lots of things, but the temptation is the same.

I don't know of a theatre, from Maine to California, that hasn't a bar connected with it, or near by. What is that bar there for?

Fallen women go to the theatres, and for no good purpose, whenever they can.

You say it is part of one's education to see good plays. Let that kind of education go to the four winds! For a child of God to help build up such an institution as the theatre of the present day is iniquitous.

A prominent and wealthy elder of a church in the West, who used to say that I was bigoted and narrow-minded and puritanical in my ideas about the stage, had a son who got married. Soon afterwards a woman came along, and put a bullet through his heart, and killed him. He had got acquainted with her at the theatre, and she claimed him. The father went trembling down to his grave a few years ago, all the sweetness of life crushed out of him.

TEMPTATION

I would rather be narrow and right, than broad and wrong. I don't want to take my two sons into a place where they will be tempted. Men are willing to be Christians now if it doesn't cost them anything, if there is no self-denial. But I wouldn't give a snap of my finger for a Christian that goes to all these places of amusement, and offsets his testimony. What we want to-day is separation from the world. It is one thing to pray God to fill you with the Spirit, but if He does, you must be separated from the world. When you want to fill a man with electricity, you have to put him on a chair with glass legs and insulate him from the earth, and then pour the electricity into him until the sparks flame from him. And if you want to get filled with the power of heaven, you'll have to get separated from the world.

If you want to get filled with the power of heaven, you'll have to get separated from the world.

You don't want your daughter or sister on the stage, do you? You wouldn't like to see your mother there. Then why patronize some one else's sister? Why encourage some one else's wife? Twenty-five thousand divorces in this country last year, and many of them the result of the theatre.

Did you ever hear of a party having a little prayer meeting before they went to a theatre? Try it, and see how you get along. Just pray that the actors may have a wonderful influence over you, and build you up, and do you a lot of good. The words would choke you.

But you say, "I know a number of good people that go."

So do I, but I know a number of people that have to

reap in their children. I have had poured into my ears, by the hundreds, tales of the untold woe and misery that has come into these families through the influence of the theatre. It is easy enough to lead your children into Sodom, but it is mighty hard to get them out. It is easy enough for the father and mother to take their children in the way of temptation, but when they want to get them away, it is a different thing.

You must be separated from the world if you want power.

But you say, "I shall lose influence."

Certainly you will. Let it go. You can't have that kind of influence and power too. Do you know the difference between influence and power? I will tell you. Ahab had influence; Elijah had power. I have never known card-playing, theatre-going, horse-racing Christians to get anybody really converted.

They talk about their immense influence. I haven't any doubt that if you had dropped down into Sodom a week before its destruction, men would have told you that Lot was the most influential man there. You would have found him sitting in the gate. He had got into office, perhaps he had been elected Judge, or Mayor of Sodom. He had got on wonderfully. He owned some of the best corner lots. Mrs. Lot moved in the highest circles. Those Sodomites would have told you he was a good deal shrewder, a far better business man than his uncle Abraham, and if he lived twenty years longer, he would be the richest of the two. A man of amazing influence! But I would like to know what *power* he had? I have an idea that when Abraham pleaded for Sodom, he thought:

"Lot has great influence in Sodom. I heard some of the people speak very highly of him when I was down there a few months ago. He has been there twenty years, and he must have got more than half a convert a year. Surely there are ten righteous men in Sodom."

But Sodom was destroyed. Lot never won a convert, but ruined his own family.

Go in for influence with the world, if you want to, but it will die when you die. Where is Ahab's influence to-day? Where is Nebuchadnezzar's influence, and the whole crowd of them, compared with Elijah's and Daniel's? Daniel has been gone these twenty-five hundred years, and still he shines, and is going to shine forever. He overcame temptation. It would have hurled him into the pit if he hadn't, and he would have gone down like those other men. He might have said:

"I shall lose rank and position if I do not eat the same kind of meat as the king does, and drink the same kind of wine. I shall lose influence."

He may have lost influence, but thank God, he got power! Can you tell who the millionaires of Babylon were? or any of the great generals? Their names have rotted with their bodies, and their influence has gone centuries ago, but Daniel lives on. Why? Because he chose to do right, and overcame temptation.

Disregard of the Sabbath

2. Another great temptation is to disregard the Sabbath.

We have a good deal worse foe than any foreign power right in our midst. This country will go to pieces if we give up the Sabbath. No country has existed a great while and been prosperous that has wiped out the Sabbath. It is easy to destroy, to tear down, but it is a thousand times better to build up.

One great means of Sabbath breaking is the bicycle.

"Oh," you say, "what is the matter with the bicycle? Isn't it a great blessing?"

Yes; and like all good blessings it can be turned into a curse by misuse. Even the Sabbath has become a curse to many. There are more cases Monday morning in the police court than any other morning of the week. When a man says, "I will leave my Sabbath-school and my church work, and take a spin in the country, and worship the God of nature," then the bicycle has become a snare, and will help bring about his ruin. I don't know what will become of the church of God if we cannot hold back the tide that is coming upon us.

> The Sabbath is easy to destroy, to tear down, but it is a thousand times better to build up.

I was in Brooklyn not long ago, and I saw something that was a revelation to me. Right opposite the church where I was to preach, a bicycle club started off for a run, at half-past ten, just as people were going to church. A few years ago that wouldn't have been countenanced in Brooklyn, the city of churches. It wasn't the scum of Brooklyn that were there, but some of the leading young men. And in that church where I preached there hardly seemed to be twenty-five young men.

Your bicycle can be a blessing, but when you go off and spend God's day in recreation, and neglect the house of God, what will become of your soul? Are you not putting yourself in the way of temptation? "Remember the Sabbath day to keep it holy." Do not turn God's holy day into a holiday.

Sunday Newspapers

3. Then there are the Sunday newspapers. I would not dare to ask how many of you read the Sunday newspapers. You think you must have them to find out the news. They have sermons, too; fine sermons. Some one took pains to look over seven of the New York Sunday papers a while ago, and this is what he found in them:

Murders and assaults, twelve columns.

Adulteries, seven columns – [first-rate Sunday reading!]

Thefts, etc., twenty-four columns.

Sporting news, eighty-one columns – [splendid Sunday reading!]

Theatrical notes, forty-four columns – [must have that for Sunday reading, you know!]

Gossip and fashion, seventy-seven columns – [your soul would get fat on that, wouldn't it?]

Sensational topics, forty-two columns – [people don't like sensational preaching, but they like forty-two columns of sensationalism in Sunday papers.]

Fiction, ninety-nine columns.

Unclean personals, eight columns – [think of a Christian man putting that paper before his children!]

Foreign news, forty-seven columns.

Political news, one hundred and thirteen columns.

Miscellaneous news, ninety-two columns.

Editorials, thirty-nine columns.

Specials, one hundred and ninety-nine columns.

Art and literature, twenty-four columns.

Religious, three and a quarter columns – [splendid sermons in Sunday papers!]

Nine hundred and eleven and a quarter columns, and only three and a quarter columns of them religious. That is Sunday reading! Gabriel himself couldn't hold an audience whose heads were full of such stuff as that. I tell you what we want is a revival that will sweep these Sunday newspapers out of our country.

There was a time when a man used to lock up his store Saturday night, and have a rest on the Sabbath. It was a time of meditation and prayer and food for his soul. But now he locks up his store, and he puts a flaming advertisement in the Sunday paper, and does a bigger business than any other day in the week. "Monday bargains." He takes up the Sunday paper to see if his advertisement is in right, and his children wait for a chance to read about the games, and the scandal that has been accumulating all the week. Then men wonder that their children are led astray. It is a wonder that more of them are not. Men, where is your conscience? I hope it will smite you the next time you offer to patronize a Sunday paper.

Yes, a man will walk right into temptation, and then wonder why he isn't kept from it. What the world needs is men who will face these issues, and stand by the right, even if he has to stand alone.

False Doctrines

4. Then there is a fourth temptation, false doctrines and false teachers.

I asked an atheist some years ago how he accounted for the creation of the world.

"Well," he said, "force and matter worked together and by chance the world came out."

That is as clear as mud to me. It is strange a man's toes are not sticking on the top of his head if things were thrown together in that way.

A man won't believe that a watch was made without a maker, but we have more absurd doctrines. Some people would have us believe nowadays that there is no matter anyway. A man thinks he exists, but he doesn't! What is to me still more awful is that they say that there is no such thing as sin. I asked a lady who held this doctrine, what she would call it if I should wilfully and in cold blood take by violence the life of another friend who was present.

> A man will walk right into temptation, and then wonder why he isn't kept from it.

"It would be an error of judgment," was her answer.

In the four years 1895-98 we had in this country 38,512 murders, while England in the same length of time had less than 600. Think of it! Less than 300 lives were lost on the Maine, and every twenty-four hours 300 in this country reel into drunkards' graves. And yet there are men and women teaching that there is no such thing as sin! O, come forward and stand against these false doctrines like men.

The temptations are all around us, but blessed is he that endureth temptation – not "Blessed is he that is tried and tempted," but "he that endureth, for when he is tried he shall receive a crown of life."

Chapter 4

Four Questions from God

I want to call your attention to four questions that God has put: the first question ever put to man, "Where art thou?" the first question ever put to woman, "What is this that thou hast done?" the question put to Cain, "Where is thy brother?" and the question put to Elijah, "What doest thou here?"

"Where Art Thou?"

A man said to me, "How do you know that God put that question to Adam?"

The best answer I can give is, Because He has put it to me many a time. I doubt whether there ever has been a son or a daughter of Adam who has not heard that voice ringing through their souls many a time. Who am I? What am I? Where am I going? So let us put the question to ourselves personally, "Where am I?" – not in the sight of man; that is of very little account; but where am I in the sight of God? – that is the question.

Adam ought to have been the first seeker. Adam ought to have gone up and down Eden crying:

"My God, my God, where art Thou? I have sinned. I have fallen."

But God, then, as now, took the place of the seeker. No man, from the time that Adam fell down to the present hour, ever thought of seeking God until God first sought for him. "The Son of Man is come to seek and to save that which was lost." I believe that the Son of Man who uttered those words is the same whose voice was heard back there in Eden, "Adam, where art thou?" For six thousand years God has been seeking for man.

In the fifteenth chapter of Luke there are three parables just to teach us that God is the seeker. It was not the sheep that was seeking the shepherd; it was the shepherd going out into the desert to hunt until he found the lost sheep. It was not that piece of silver seeking the woman; it was the woman seeking for the lost piece of silver. Those parables are given to teach us that God is the great Seeker. If you can discover yourself and find out who you are, and what you are, that will be the greatest discovery you can ever make. That is what the prodigal did when he came to himself – he found out who he was.

Most of us live away from home. We are hiding as Adam did in the bushes of Eden. There was a time when God's voice thrilled Adam's soul with joy and gladness, and he thrilled God's heart with joy. They lived in sweet fellowship with each other. God had lifted Adam to the very gates of heaven, and had made him lord over all creation. I haven't a doubt that He had plans to raise Adam still higher – higher than the angels, higher than seraphim and cherubim, higher than Gabriel, who stands in the presence of Jehovah, and Michael, the archangel. But the man turned and became a traitor to Him who wanted to bless him.

What Hast Thou Done?

Now look for a moment to see what God said to the woman. "What is this that thou has done?"

What had she done? She had disobeyed. She had turned from the fountain of life to the fountain of death, and drank from that fountain. She had introduced sin into this world, and God let her live long enough on the face of the earth to see what she had done. The first child that was born after the fall was a murderer. Bear in mind that sin leaped into this world full grown. The woman had gained for herself a fallen nature, and she transmitted it to her posterity. She lived nearly a thousand years if she lived as long as Adam, and had a chance to see something of the untold woe and misery she had introduced into this world.

Look at the wretchedness and agony caused by sin in all our great cities! We don't have to go back into history or into other lands to see what Eve did when she introduced sin into this world.

"What hast thou done?" It was a terrible thing to turn away from the living God to the enemy of all righteousness; but, thank God, right then and there

He put a lamp of promise in her hand. The only ray of hope that shone forth for two thousand years, as far as we know, was the hope God gave then when He said that He would put enmity between the woman's seed and the serpent, and while it should bruise His heel, He should bruise the serpent's head. Thank God for that promise!

Jesus Christ, the purest being who ever came to this earth to save mankind, was crucified. I believe if Gabriel should come down from heaven with all the glory of that upper world, and try to save men, they would try to blacken his character inside of a week. The ungodly do not like the godly. The impure do not like the pure. There is enmity still. Men may cavil and discuss as much as they like, but there is the fact. God's prediction is fulfilled. The serpent shall have its head bruised, and every man of us should do all he can to bruise it. Our worst enemy is sin.

Where Is Thy Brother?

But I come to the third question: "Where is thy brother?"

Here is a young man. He is the only son of a widowed mother, whose husband died and left her bankrupt. She has toiled hard to give her son an education. She has watched over him with the tenderest care, and he leaves home with high hopes of being a comfort and blessing to that mother in her declining years. He has gone down to college, and, as is so often said, he is "easily influenced." If he is easily influenced for *bad*, why not for *good*? Somebody has tempted him, and has led him into sins of which he had never dreamed. He has fallen into the depths of wickedness, and is fast reaping the wages of sin.

Many a young man has gone from a home like that, and before his college course has closed has been put into his coffin and sent back to his mother.

Where is thy brother? Where is he? Is your answer going to be like that of Cain: "Am I my brother's keeper? What is that to me? I have nothing to do with Abel. I shift the responsibility. I deny that I am responsible for anyone. I mind my own business, and let every man mind his. I am not going to take any interest in that man"?

In a western city, some years ago, they tried to get a very influential merchant to throw his influence against the saloon. He was a temperance man and had a lovely family, but he thought it might affect his business if he should identify himself with prohibitionists. He had influence enough to have carried that town for no license; but he said it was none of his business, and would not interfere. The town voted for license.

A few months later he went to the station, with his carriage and his footman, to get his wife and daughter, who were coming from the East. The train failed to arrive, and soon it flashed over the wires that there had been a wreck, and that this man's wife and daughter were dead. When they came to make an investigation they found that the engineer was drunk.

Was it none of that man's business whether or not liquor was sold?

Some years ago a man living on the banks of a lake, one cold night when the thermometer was below zero, heard a cry of distress. A man out skating had gone through the ice, and it is supposed that he had got hold of the ice, and kept his head above the water, and called for help. The man heard his cries, but said:

"It is none of my business. It is a cold night, and I don't want to get up and go out. No one had any business to go out there skating, anyway."

The cries became fainter and fainter, and finally ceased. The next day the body was found. The man was foolish enough to tell what he had heard, and that whole population rose up in indignation and hounded him out of town. They said he wasn't fit to live among them.

Every one would say, "That is true"; and yet is he any worse than one who will see a young man go down through drink, and not lift his hand to help him? Where is thy brother?

There is a story told of a great storm on the coast. The life boat was being manned, and a mother came rushing down to the shore to find that her boy was going out in it. She cried:

"My boy, it will kill me to have you go. You know you are all I have left. Willie was lost at sea. Don't, go."

But there was the wreck out there, and men on the wreck, and he felt compelled to go and rescue his fellow men. The mother saw that boat rise and fall on the billows, and it seemed as if the storm would dash it to pieces, and all would be lost.

At last they reached the wreck, and rescued the men. That mother listened, and looked out into the storm that seemed to be raging harder and harder. By and by the boat came near enough so that the son could call to his mother. He put his hand to his mouth, and cried:

"Mother, I've saved Willie!"

His own brother, whom they thought was lost, was on board.

Oh friends, have you ever tried to save anyone? I do not ask you if you have *succeeded*, but have you ever *tried*? God pity the man who never tried to save anyone! God pity him! If you haven't, make up your mind to-day that you will do it. Wouldn't you like to have the joy that they have in heaven over someone that repents? What a grand day this would be if you could be the instrument in God's hands of turning someone from darkness to light, and from the power of sin unto God!

You can join with Cain and say, "Am I my brother's keeper?" But, thank God, you can do something better than that. You can say, "By the help of God I will save someone, and my life shall not be a failure."

I was on the *Spree* when the shaft broke and knocked a hole in the ship's bottom. The stern sank thirty feet in mid ocean, and for a whole week, if a storm had burst upon us, we would have gone down. One man was so bewildered and terrified that he jumped overboard. I remember how wretched I felt to think I couldn't help him, to see him left out there in mid ocean, head above the waves, looking at us. The passengers took life preservers and whatever they could find, and threw them to him, but all fell short. I never forgot the look of that man; it has followed me all these years. But what would you have said of me, if the life-line had laid right at my feet and I had refused to throw it to him? What would you say?

O, friends, the life-line lies at our feet. Men are sinking all around us. Let us throw out the life-line!

A father was told one day by a friend that his boy had got into bad company and was drinking. The father wouldn't believe a word of it, and was quite indignant with the man for telling him. But one night he thought he would wait until his son came in. It came to the small hours of the morning – it was a cold night in winter – and he heard someone trying to get the key into the door; he went to the door and found that it was his boy, drunk. He shut the door in his face and told him never to come back to that house; he was a disgrace to him.

Then he went to bed and tried to sleep, but his conscience rose up and smote him. The thought came, "Have I ever tried to save my boy? I have often put strong drink before him on my table. Have I ever talked to him about a better life? Have I ever told him of a Savior?"

The man got up and dressed himself, and went out that cold night. He found the policeman on that beat, and hunted until he found the drunken son, and brought him home. When the boy was sober the father confessed that he hadn't done right himself, and asked his boy to forgive him. The result was that the boy was saved.

Do you know of anyone that is stumbling over you? You have been a professed Christian for many years, and you never have spoken to anyone about his soul. You have seen them go down all around you. Where is thy brother? Perhaps a letter written to him to-day may save him. Ask him to forgive you for not having spoken to him before, for not throwing out the life-line before. If he is easily influenced, say:

"God helping me, I will influence him to be good and to be right."

What Doest Thou Here?

Elijah was out of communion with God. Elijah that was once so bold had become a coward. Elijah that had been up to this hour so successful, had taken his eyes off of his Master, and had fled out into the desert and sat down under the juniper tree and wished himself dead.

Some of you may have become discouraged and disheartened. You haven't had the success that you expected to have in Christian work. You have got your eyes off of the Master, and you have fled out into the desert, and you are trying to live a sort of hermit life. My dear friends, what we want, it seems to me, is to get right into the heat of battle and stay there until the Master calls us home. I would rather die than to outlive my usefulness. I would rather have the summons come right now than to live and not to be used of God. I cannot conceive of a greater calamity coming upon Elijah, the man that had been so wonderfully used, than to die there discouraged and disheartened. I would like to die in the harness.

One of Scotland's great preachers has brought out this thought:

"The wanderer was alone, yet not alone. A voice he could neither mistake nor misinterpret had sounded in his ears the thrilling question, 'What doest thou here, Elijah?' Every syllable was pregnant with meaning and with rebuke. 'What *doest* thou here?' Life (and none should know better than thee) is a great *doing*; not hermit inaction, inglorious repose. 'What doest *thou*?' – thou, my vicegerent in these degenerate days – thou whom I have honored above thy fellows, and who hast had proof upon proof of my faithfulness? 'What doest thou *here*' – here in this desolate spot; away from duty; the Baal altars rebuilding; my own altar in ruins; the sword of persecution unsheathed, and the bleating flock left by thee, coward shepherd, to the ravening wolf? 'What doest thou here, *Elijah*?' Thy very name rebukes thee! Where is God, thy strength? Where are the prayers and vows of Carmel? Child of weakness, belying thy name and destiny, '*What – doest – thou – here?*'"

> If God calls you to some service, do not stop to discuss whether it is a higher service or not.

At this time Elijah missed the opportunity of his life; it never returned to him again. God permitted him to cast his mantle on Elisha, but when he came to the very place where God would have used him mightily, he fled like a coward. Many of us miss grand opportunities. If God calls you to some service, do not stop to discuss whether it is a higher service or not; leave that to Him. If God calls you, say, "Here am I; send me."

"What doest thou here?" Are you out of communion with God? Has some cursed sin come in and separated you from God, and your life is like a blasted tree in the desert without any power? If so, ask Him to forgive you. Return with your whole heart unto Him, and He will use you mightily.

Chapter 5

The Transfiguration

It is a singular fact that John, the only one of the four evangelists that was with Christ on the Mount of Transfiguration, is the only one who does not give an account of it. Perhaps the reason is that the scene was so solemn, so impressive, and so holy that he could not bring himself to write of it. Peter, who was also present, barely mentioned it in his writings that have come down to us. His only reference to the scene is in his second epistle, written many years afterwards, when he was an old man:

"We were eye witnesses of His majesty; for He received from God the Father honor and glory, when there came such a voice to Him from the excellent glory, This is my beloved Son, in whom I am well pleased. And this voice, which came from heaven, we heard when we were with Him in the holy mount."

There are scenes in our lives that we never like to mention in public. There are times when God comes so near to us that we feel that others won't understand if we tell them of it. I believe that the reason why Christ told His disciples not to refer to His transfiguration until after His resurrection was that the people would not believe that they had had such a revelation.

Before and After

It is a good thing to see what happened just before this wonderful scene, and also what followed. In Matthew's account (16:24-28) we read:

> "Then said Jesus unto His disciples, if any man will come after me, let him deny himself, and take up his cross, and follow me. For whosoever will save his life shall lose it; and whosoever will lose his life for my sake shall find it. For what is a man profited, if he shall gain the whole world, and lose his own soul? Or what shall a man give in exchange for his soul? For the Son of man shall come in the glory of His Father with His angels; and then He shall reward every man according to his works. Verily I say unto you, There be some standing here, which shall not taste of death, till they see the Son of man coming in His kingdom."

Then He takes them up into the mountain, and the transfiguration scene follows. First, the cross, then the transfiguration, and after that, service, when they came down and found the boy possessed with an evil spirit.

When God gave Moses the law at Sinai, there were thunders and lightnings, and the mount was altogether on a smoke because Jehovah descended upon it in fire. Whatever touched the mount – man or beast – was to be put to death. But here Christ took His three beloved disciples with Him, and was manifested before them in glory and peace.

Men of Prayer

Jesus took Peter and John and James, and went up into a mountain to pray. Every one of the six men who met on that mountain was eminently a man of prayer. And it was while Christ was praying that His face and His garments were changed, and became shining as the sun and white as the light. Then there appeared and talked with Him two men, Moses and Elijah. Many of us have seen people whose very countenances have been changed after a season of prayer, and their whole lives have seemed to be transformed. I believe that is how Moses got his shining face when he had been in communion with God for forty days. We cannot be in real communion with God without getting more or less of that same glory. When Andrew Bonar was in America, after Major Whittle had been speaking once on the shining face of Stephen, Dr. Bonar said:

> We cannot be in real communion with God without getting more or less of that same glory.

"Did you ever notice that when the Jews accused Stephen of blasphemy against Moses' law, God lit up Stephen's face with the same glory that He had given to the face of Moses?"

When men are brought into communion with God, He will cause their faces to shine.

Famous Councils

There have been some famous councils in the history of the world.

I remember the excitement when Lincoln and Grant and Stevenson (vice-president of the Confederacy) and one or two others met on the James river at the close of the war to agree on terms. I was near by at the time. The whole nation was breathless to hear the results of that conference, which would mean so much to a country that had already been wasted with years of bloodshed. Every newspaper was eager to find out what was to be the outcome.

I remember also the excitement in all Europe in 1878 when representatives of the different powers met at Berlin to adjust the Eastern question. The results of that council meant peace or war to all the powers represented.

Earlier in the century, Napoleon of France and Alexander of Russia met at Tilsit, after a long and bloody struggle, to settle terms of peace and re-arrange the map of Europe. We are told that, jealous of each other's dignity, they must meet in mid-stream between the two opposing armies; so a gorgeous raft, richly carpeted and beautifully furnished, was built and moored in the river, and in the midst of these evidences of earthly pomp and with the eyes of all Europe upon them, the two monarchs met.

We can recall other critical councils in the history of the world, when the destiny of nations hung in the balance. But never was there held so important a council as this on the Mount of Transfiguration.

There was none of the glamor and grandeur of earthly councils; but the bare hilltop was lit up with the glory of another world.

No one was there whom this world held high in rank and honor; but Moses was there, who was greater than Pharaoh and all the gods of Egypt; and Elijah, mightier than Ahab and all the priests of Baal; Peter and James and John, who were to be the founders of an organization that should embrace the whole world; and the Son of God was there, who is King of Kings and Lord of Lords.

The question discussed was not of peace and war between conflicting nations, but of peace between God and man, of reconciliation between heaven and earth, of the opening up of a way for fallen man to return to his Father's home. Moses and Elias appeared and talked with Christ of "His decease which He should accomplish at Jerusalem." Matthew and Mark leave out that sentence, but Luke gives us the subject of their conversation. Men like to talk about what they think the most about, and these men evidently thought more of that event than of anything else that was ever going to take place upon earth. It was nine months before the death of Jesus, and they spoke of that; the shadow of the cross appearing on the Mount of Transfiguration.

Asleep

Peter and the others were heavy with sleep; but when they were awake they saw His glory and the two men that stood with Him. I have often thought that those three disciples represent the church of to-day. They fell asleep just before the glory burst upon that scene. It seems as if we are coming near to the consummation of things; that the glory of the Son of Man is about to be manifested; and yet the bride is falling asleep, instead of watching for the coming of the Bridegroom. Then, as Moses and Elijah were about to depart, Peter said: "Master, it is good for us to be here; and let us make three tabernacles, one for thee, and one for Moses, and one for Elias, not knowing what he said. While he thus spake, there came a cloud, and overshadowed them, and they feared as they entered into the cloud. And there came a voice out of the cloud, saying, This is my beloved Son, hear Him. And when the voice was past Jesus was found alone. And they kept it close and told no man in those days any of those things which they had seen."

Three Dispensations

We may say that three dispensations were represented on that mountain – the law, the prophets, and the gospel.

When God called Moses to go down into Egypt to service, notice how hard he tried to be excused. He made one excuse after another. How many of you have been trying to excuse yourselves from doing what God would have you do?

Did you ever think what Moses would have lost if God had excused him and let Aaron, or Caleb, or Joshua, or some one else take his place? He never would have been on that mountain with Christ fifteen hundred years afterward. Didn't God reward him a million times over for all the hardships he endured in the wilderness? And yet here are men and women to-day trying to be excused from God's service.

Elijah was another man of prayer; a man who knew God intimately. Like Moses, he had been forty days alone with God. These two men probably knew more about God, and more about man, than any one in their day or generation.

You remember how Elijah got under that juniper tree and wanted God to kill him. He was fleeing from Jezebel, and wanted to die. I imagine that when he was on the Mount of Transfiguration he said:

"Oh, I am so glad the Lord didn't answer my prayer, and let me die under that juniper tree."

The other three men, Peter and James and John, were to take up the work that Christ was to leave, in this new dispensation.

Great Men Not Appreciated

I can just imagine when Peter wanted to make three tabernacles, and keep Moses and Elias there, he would have said, if he had dared:

"I wish, Moses, that you would go down to Jerusalem and preach. How the city would be stirred!"

A man has got to be dead about a thousand years before he is appreciated. Ask a man in Noah's day to name a great man, and he would say, "Enoch." Noah would have been nobody. Ask a man in Abraham's day who was the greatest man, and he would not have answered "Abraham," but "Noah." In Moses' day it would have been Abraham, in Elijah's day Moses, and in John the Baptist's day Elijah.

Here, on the mount, was a man that was to be used perhaps more than any man that has ever lived in winning people to Christ; and that man was Peter. But there wasn't a man in the city of Jerusalem that thought he amounted to anything. He was an unlettered man; but he knew the Lord Jesus. He thought that if he could only get Elijah and Moses to go down to Jerusalem and hold some evangelistic meetings; if Moses would only go down and thunder out the law; if Elijah would go and tell the people how the prophecies had all been fulfilled in Christ, how it would stir the whole city! Yet the man to do that mighty work was not Moses or Elijah, it was Peter himself. He did a greater work than Moses, a greater work than Elijah, a greater work in winning souls than even his Master, for Jesus said, "Greater works than these shall ye do."

God may use you more than any one who has yet lived in your day. I believe that if we hunger and thirst for power in God's service above everything else, God will not disappoint us. The idea that others can be more used than we ourselves has been the great hindrance to the church in all ages.

No Introduction Needed

Notice, too, that these men had not lost their identity. Moses had been gone fifteen hundred years, and Elijah had been gone one thousand years, and yet they were pretty well known. I don't believe that the Lord had to say to Peter, James and John,

"This is Moses, and this Elias."

I believe they knew them without any introduction.

I think that when I see my Master I shall know Him.

Do you ask, How?

I don't know.

I heard of a child whose mother died so early that she could not remember the mother. She did not have a photograph, and never saw her face. After she had come to years of understanding, she was taken sick, and when she was dying, suddenly her face lit up, she seemed to see her mother, and said:

"O mother!"

So I believe that we shall know Moses and Elijah just as those apostles did on that mountain. Let us remember that if we do Christ's work, and are identified with Him, the time will come when we shall see the King face to face, and be with Him forever.

God Spake

Now, notice another thing. God the Father spoke on that occasion. It is supposed by Bible students that for four thousand years God never said that He was well pleased, from the time of creation before Adam fell, until the second Adam made His appearance on the banks of the Jordan. But when Jesus came up out of Jordan, then God could say again that He was well pleased, and He broke the silence of four thousand years. Here on the Mount of Transfiguration He adds another word:

"This is my beloved Son, hear Him."

Moses had come to hand over his commission. The law was fulfilled by Jesus Christ; his work was done. There was a greater than Moses on that mountain, although Peter, John and James may not have believed it at that time. The Jews looked upon Christ as an impostor, as a blasphemer, and wanted to sweep Him from the face of the earth. His disciples may have wavered sometimes, and wondered if He were the true Messiah. This whole scene may have been to convince these three men beyond all doubt that Jesus was the long-looked-for Messiah. God spoke again from heaven and said:

"Hear my Son. The law and the prophets are fulfilled, and the work of Moses and Elijah is done."

Like the moon and the stars, which fade away, their

light eclipsed by the rising sun, so Moses and Elijah now pass into obscurity, for their work is accomplished.

Moses may have represented the dead saints. He died, and God buried him. And Elijah, who was caught up in a chariot of fire, may have represented the living saints that will be alive when Christ returns.

The Shekinah glory, the voice of God, the law and the prophets were here united in testifying to Christ.

If Jesus Had Gone!

Mr. Spurgeon draws a very vivid picture of this scene. He says: "When the cloud came and received Moses and Elijah out of sight, and they were taken back into the other world, what would have been the result if Jesus Christ had gone, too?" What a dark night it would have been if our Lord and Master had been caught up with Moses and Elijah, and no Christ had died for our sins. Oh, how Jesus Christ lit up this world! But suppose that Christ had gone up to heaven on the other side of Calvary, and had never finished His work. Suppose that God in His love for His Son had said:

> The longer I live the more I am convinced that what this world wants is Jesus Christ.

"I can't let those men spit upon you and smite you; I will take you back to my bosom."

What darkness would have settled down on this world! But Moses disappeared, and Elijah disappeared, and Christ only was left, for Christ is all. The law and the prophets were honored and fulfilled in Him.

My dear friends, the longer I live the more I am convinced that what this world wants is Jesus Christ. If we preach Him more, live Him more, and love Him more, and let Him be constantly held up to this lost world, we shall accomplish something. All our work that is separate from Christ will be just hay, wood, stubble and chaff; it will be burned up, when God comes to test our works. What we want is to be out of sight ourselves, so that when people see us they won't think of us, but of Christ. We must decrease, but He must increase. When Peter wanted to put Christ on a level with Moses and Elijah, then it was that God the Father took them away. Jesus Christ has no peers; there is no one to be compared to Him. He excels the lawgiver and all the prophets. His name is above every other name under heaven.

No Compromise

If you want power with God, just get as far from the world as you can. Suppose that Peter had said:

"Lord, if we go down from this mount, can we play cards just as much as ever, and dance just as much as ever? Because we have been in this mount with you, and had such holy visions, have we got to give up all these things?"

Could you conceive of such a thing? It seems to me that if we get one look at Christ in His love and beauty, this world and its pleasures will look very small to us. We must be out-and-out for Christ, so that there will be no compromise. The cross of Christ is suffering more to-day by people trying to serve the god of this world and the God of this Bible at the same time, than from anything else. Get near to Christ, and you will never want to go back to the world. People may call you narrow, but God uses a narrow man and a narrow woman.

Work after Worship

One thing more: I can sympathize with Peter, for I should like to have been there myself. I should like to have spent a month there, and let Elijah tell me about all the things he had been interested in. Wouldn't that have been splendid? I should like very much to have heard Moses tell of his experiences. But there was a work down below the mountain, and while it is delightful to get a glimpse of the coming glory, there is work to be done. At a conference a young minister who had been in Palestine used to take every chance he could get to tell about what he saw there. He got to be quite a nuisance. At last Bishop Ames got up and said:

"Brother, I would rather be five minutes with Christ, than to be five years where He has been."

As these men went down from that mountain, they met a father who had a son possessed with a devil. When the father went to bring his son to Jesus the devil tripped him up. Like a bad tenant, he tried to do as much harm as he could before leaving. The devil knew that he was going to get orders to get out, and so gave the boy such a throw that he nearly killed him. The disciples could not cast the devil out. The boy was deaf and dumb, and I presume the disciples said:

"Oh, you know, that is a hopeless case. If he could only tell us how he feels, or if we could only shout into his ear, we might get at him; but we cannot make him hear or speak, and we cannot do anything."

They lacked faith. But the Lord came down, and that father came to Christ. "Mark you," Spurgeon says, "he [the father] was a poor theologian when he came to Christ. He came and said, 'If thou canst do anything,' and the Lord rebuked him right there. He said, 'If thou canst believe.' He put the 'if' in the right place. 'All things are possible to him that believeth; bring him unto me.'"

You may have some brother or father or friend whom you want to be converted. You have brought them to Christians, and the devil has not been cast out. Listen! What did Christ say to his father? "Bring him unto Me."

There is a great deal of joy in the thought that Christ has power over the devils. Remember that "all power in heaven and earth" is given to Him, and don't think for a moment that any man is beyond the reach of God's mercy. Don't you think that your brother who is a slave to strong drink is beyond the reach of God. "Bring him to Me," says Christ. Get beyond your church, your society, and go right to the Master Himself.

When that mother came and told Elisha that her child was dead, the prophet said to his servant, "Take that stick and lay it out on that dead child." Away went the servant. But that woman was wiser than Elisha; she would not leave him. She was not going to trust in that staff or that servant, she wanted the prophet himself. Some people think that it will do to work for Christ without giving *themselves* to the work. No. Sometimes our whole life must be given to win a person. Make up your mind that if it costs you your life you are going to do it. When the child was thrown on the ground as if dead, Jesus *took him by the hand*, and lifted him up. The touch of love and sympathy is what most men need.

Looking Earthward

I heard once of a man who dreamed that he was swept into heaven, and he was there in the glory world, and, oh! he was so delighted to think that he had at last made heaven. All at once one came and said:

"Come, I want to show you something."

He took him to the battlements, and said, "Look down yonder; what do you see?"

"I see a very dark world."

"Look and see if you know it."

"Why, yes," he said, "that is the world I have come from."

"What do you see?"

"Why, men are blindfolded there. Many of them are going over a precipice."

"Well, will you stay here and enjoy heaven, or will you go back to earth and spend a little longer time, and tell those men about this world?"

He was a worker who had been discouraged, like Elijah. He awoke from his sleep, and later said:

"I have never wished myself dead since."

Do not wish to be always abiding in idleness on the Mount of Transfiguration, but go down into the world and bring souls to the Master. It is good to be on the mountain top, in spiritual communion, and occupied *with* Jesus; but it is not good to remain there – we must descend to the plain, and be occupied *for* Jesus in everyday life.

Chapter 6

Mary and Martha

Mary of Bethany is one of the most famous women in history, and yet there is very little that she ever did that the world would call great. I can find only ten words recorded that fell from her lips. We are not told that she was beautiful, or that she was accomplished; we are quite sure that she never went to any college, or spoke from any platform; we do not know that she ever exhorted or led a Bible class. Nothing of that kind is told of her, and yet she is one of the most famous women of history.

All four evangelists have something to say about Mary. In the 10th chapter of Luke we first catch sight of her. In that chapter Christ sent out His seventy disciples. They came back jubilant, and He checked their spirit and told them to rejoice that their names were written in heaven. A little further on we come to a practical kind of religion, in the story of the good Samaritan. Then we come to Mary, who would probably be considered by many who like the good Samaritan, as a very impractical woman.

Our first glimpse of the home at Bethany is a very humiliating scene. Martha brings a complaint against her sister. Picture the company gathered there: Christ and His apostles are sitting with Mary, when Martha bursts into the room with a complaint against her sister. Luke 10:38-42 –

> "Now it came to pass, as they went, that He entered into a certain village: and a certain woman, named Martha, received Him into her house. And she had a sister called Mary, which also sat at Jesus' feet, and heard His word. But Martha was cumbered about much serving, and came to Him and said, Lord, dost Thou not care that my sister hath left me to serve alone? Bid her therefore, that she help me." Now comes the rebuke: "And Jesus answered and said unto her, Martha, Martha, thou art careful and troubled about many things, but one thing is needful: and Mary hath chosen that good part, which shall not be taken away from her."

This homeless Preacher had come into that home to light it up, and He made it one of the most famous homes in all history. Jesus rebuked Martha. I do not doubt for a moment that she was a follower of Jesus as well as Mary. They both loved the Savior. Martha had received Him into her home, and it might have been that she was the first of that family to receive Christ into her heart; but the two sisters were unlike each other. One wanted to *do*, to *serve*; the other wanted to *receive* from Christ that she might serve Him better.

There was another difference between those two sisters, and I think I can best explain by telling you an incident in my own life.

I was going through Chicago once, when a prominent man called upon me, sat down at the table by my side, and said,

"Mr. Moody, I want you to help me"; and the tears rolled down his cheeks.

I said, "What! is it possible that you have lost your hope?"

"No," he said.

"Are you not still superintendent of that large Sabbath School?"

"Yes."

"And are you not in good standing in your church?"

"Yes."

"Is there any known sin that has come into your life and separated you from God?"

"No."

"Then," I said, "what do you want?"

"Well," he said, "the fact is, my wife has something that I haven't got. She has something that keeps her in perfect peace, and I have to hold on all the time to keep my religion. And now," he said, "I want you to help me."

That was the difference between those two sisters. Both loved Christ, but Martha was one of these fretful, anxious, worried women, a little out of temper now and then. Are you acquainted with any like her? I think that we meet about ten thousand Marthas to one Mary.

A great many people seem to think that to be irritable is nothing very serious, and are apt to excuse themselves by saying that they are tired and overworked. I haven't any doubt but that was true in regard to Martha. A good many Christian workers are overworked, but that is no excuse for losing one's temper.

A prominent London clergyman made the statement a few years ago that he hadn't been ruffled in his temper for twenty years. I thought that was a most extraordinary thing for a man that had a large parish right in the heart of London, and so many curates and co-workers; a public man pulled and hauled in all directions. I had a talk with him, and a gentleman was there who said,

"I think that Mr. Moody ought to be excused because he has so much on hand."

"Not a bit of it," said the clergyman; "no man ought to undertake so much Christian work that it wears him out, and makes him irritable and fretful."

I confess that I did have so many things on hand that I used to let little things annoy me. Now, that was Martha exactly. It is a habit that grows upon people. I know some Christians who are so irritable and so impatient that it is pretty hard to get on with them.

A mother was baking one day, and her little child that was nearer her heart, probably, than anyone else in the world, came up to the table and took hold of the basin and tipped the dough on the floor. The mother struck the child, and said she was always in her way. Only a few weeks after the child sickened, and when she was delirious she said,

"Mother, will I be in the way of the angels?"

Do you think the mother ever forgave herself for that harsh word and angry act?

I remember hearing of a little child that had gone out into the field and picked a bouquet of wild flowers, that she wanted to bring to her mother. Her mother was talking with a neighbor when she came, and the little thing came running up and said:

"Mamma, mamma, these flowers are for you!"

The mother said, "Hush, child, I am talking."

But the little child pulled at her mother's dress again and said, "They are for you, mamma," and her heart was full of joy to think she had brought a little bouquet to her mother. The mother pushed the child away, and because she cried the mother put her into a dark closet to punish her.

That is what the child got for bringing a little bouquet to its mother!

It doesn't seem of much importance that we are sometimes irritable in the home; but what effect will it have on your family?

Sins of Women

Now I honestly believe that this is the great sin of women. We men are guilty of this and many other sins, and our prisons are full of men. Women stay at home more than the men, and it is mostly in the home life that women sin. Many have such a habit of quick, sharp speaking. A woman's tongue is sometimes very sharp, and it cuts, it stings. I believe that was the trouble with Martha. It was very unkind of her to come in before that company of men, and enter a complaint against Mary. Don't you think that she ought to have had more self-control? Would Christ have rebuked her if she had not been wrong? That rebuke has come down nineteen hundred years:

"Martha, Martha, thou art troubled about many things."

We must stop worrying and fretting if we want real power with God and with man.

Some gentlemen were discussing which one of these sisters would make the better wife, and one said that he would prefer "Martha before dinner, and Mary after dinner." I beg to differ with him; give me Mary all the time. If I had to eat a dinner that was prepared by a fretful, irritable woman, it would not taste half so sweet. I think Mary is a good deal better all around.

Off to Hear Christ

I can imagine that Mary was in the habit of slipping off to the temple very often to hear Christ. Whenever He came into the city, she was there. Martha would remonstrate. She would say,

"Monday, this is wash day. We must have our washing done anyway."

But Mary would say, "Christ won't be here long. He will soon be gone from Jerusalem, and I am going to get all I can from Him."

And it may be one Monday that Martha stayed at home and did the work, and Mary slipped over into the temple, and came back and told Martha that she had heard Christ say, "Come unto me all ye that labor and are heavy laden, and I will give you rest." Wasn't that better than attending to the washing? I would say, let the washing go for a little while, if I could get such a feast of fat things.

Then Tuesday, ironing day; and Martha remonstrates again, but Mary must go. She must get all that she can. She was going to drink deep because she needed it. It is a great thing to drink from Christ's fullness when you can, so that when the time comes that you need grace you will have it, and your soul will be kept in perfect peace and perfect rest.

> I do not think that Mary was a shirk. Jesus never made people lazy, and never will.

I do not think that Mary was a shirk. Jesus never made people lazy, and never will. Perhaps when Mary came back from the temple she may have sat up late at night to help Martha with the mending, or she may have risen early and done some of the ironing.

I don't believe she made it any harder for Martha by following Christ. If you are really serving Him you don't make it any harder for those around you; you will help them and save them work in every way you can. I like what Mr. Morgan says about this. He says that the "also" in verse thirty-nine – "which *also* sat at Jesus' feet" – means that Mary did her share of the work and *in addition* sat at Jesus' feet. She hurried her work, perhaps, that she might have time to be with the Master.

Dangers of Overwork

Now another thing: It may be that Martha not only overworked, but did not take care of her health. Some people get so interested in the Lord's work that they don't eat and sleep regularly.

I met a city missionary who was the most jaded person I had seen for a long time. She looked as if she hadn't a friend in the world; her life was nearly all gone.

I said: "I hope you are blessed in your work."

"Oh, yes," she said, "it is a blessed work."

"I hope you enjoy it."

"Yes," she said, "but I get so tired."

"What, tired *of* the work or tired *in* it?"

"Oh, never tired of the work, but I do get tired in it."

I said, "I don't think that Christ is a hard master, or wants His children to get worn out. Do you take one day out of seven to rest?"

"Oh, no, we never think of that! Thirteen of us are employed by a wealthy lady who thinks that because we are doing the Lord's work we don't need any rest for the body."

That is a great mistake. This woman worked thirteen or fourteen hours a day, seven days in the week, and of course her body was worn out. When the body gets tired the mind gets tired, and then we are apt to become irritable. So it is very important that we take good care

MARY AND MARTHA

of the body. Very often people get into a nervous state simply for the lack of food and sleep.

Do you remember that Elijah got under that juniper tree and laid down and wished himself dead? There was God's representative on earth, the man that stood nearer to the throne of God than any man on the face of the earth at that time, wishing himself dead! An angel came and woke him up, and said, "Rise and eat," and there was a cake there on the coals and a cruse of water, and he got refreshed. After he got refreshed, he fell asleep again. I presume he hadn't had any sleep for days and nights; perhaps hadn't had any food; he was so full of zeal. The zeal of the Lord was just eating him right up. He had another sleep, and the angel woke him up again and said, "Rise and eat," and he rose, and there was a cake that had been cooked, and a cruse of water. The Lord didn't upbraid him *then*; the Lord didn't test him *then*. He fed him and got him rested, and then when He got him off into Horeb, He said, "Elijah, what doest thou here?" Then God took him in hand and dealt with him; but He fed him first and got him rested.

I think very often Christians get into a nervous state when they need food and sleep. In these days of rush and bustle, people think the world can't get on without them. That is like Martha. She thought that whole house depended upon her, and things must be done in time; and when Jesus came to the house He must have the very best dinner that could be gotten up in all Bethany; and while she was fretting and worrying and getting the dinner, Mary was just sitting at His feet, drinking in of His fullness until her soul was refreshed.

Now there are two dangers you want to keep in mind. If you are active and neglect communion, it won't be long before you get into Martha's state. You are sure to get there; it is inevitable. Then there may be so much communion that you neglect to be practical. That is another danger. If we want real peace and joy, we must keep the two together. We must be practical, and yet we must have communion. I have yet to find a Christian worker in this or any other country that has had success any length of time that has neglected communion. You don't lose anything by going away alone every day, and having a little season with God alone. That is where you get strength, that is where you get power.

> You don't lose anything by having a little season with God alone. That is where you get strength.

And it is not only to go apart to pray. Some people say to me,

"You know, Mr. Moody, I pray, but after I have prayed five minutes my mind wanders and goes off in all directions; I can't pray more than four or five minutes at a time, and hold my thoughts."

Well, there is something that is higher than that. When we are really communing, it is not only our talking to God, but God talking to us. Do you think that Moses was up in the mountain forty days and forty nights praying to God all the time? No flesh and blood could stand that. I can imagine during those forty days and forty nights Moses asked God a great many questions, and God answered a great many. I think that if God should take me up into a mountain and talk with me, I should ask Him a great many questions; and I have no doubt that during those forty days Moses asked God a great many questions. God talked to Moses, took him into His secret pavilion, and told him the history of the world. I do not believe he would have ever written those five books if he hadn't had those days and nights in the mountain with God. And what days and nights they must have been! That is when he came down with a shining face. His face was lit up with the glory of that upper world.

I believe that Mary asked Jesus a great many questions, and that He told her a great many secrets. Perhaps she learned many things that even the disciples didn't know. All the disciples, as someone has said, were very near Christ, but the seventy that He sent out were nearer than the rest, and the twelve were nearer than the seventy, and the three, Peter, James and John, were nearer than the twelve. But I have an idea that Mary was nearer than any of them. Those men were constantly discussing who should be the greatest, but Mary had no thought of being the greatest. In Jesus' estimation she may have been the greatest because she only sought to sit at His feet like a little child, and learn of Him, and obey Him.

Mary In Trouble

Mary's communion with Jesus brought her so near to His heart that when the time of trouble came she knew where to go for comfort. A great many people do not learn that secret in prosperity, and so when the billows come rolling up against them, they don't know which way to turn. The darkest and most wretched place on the face of the earth, I think, is a home where death has entered, but where Christ is unknown. They have no hope of a resurrection, no hope of a brighter day coming.

I can imagine that one day Lazarus came into the house with a hot, burning fever in his head, and said to his two sisters:

"I am afraid that I have a fever." Perhaps a fever that had taken away the father and mother a little while before.

His sisters were greatly alarmed. Everything was done to break up that fever, but in vain. Then they send off into the city of Jerusalem for their family physician, but his remedies also fail. At last the doctor comes out of that sick chamber – many of us have traveled this road – and shakes his head, and says:

"There is no hope."

Lazarus is going to leave them, and Mary's first thought is, Where is Jesus of Nazareth? They never needed Him more than at that very hour. It is said of Jonathan Edwards that when dying of small-pox, he said:

"Where is my old friend, Jesus of Nazareth?"

My friends, the hour is coming when you will need Him. Mark that! You may think that you can get on very well without Him now, but the hour is surely coming when you will need Him. The hour had come when Mary and Martha needed Him as a comforter.

They called a messenger and sent him off to find Jesus. Perhaps he hadn't been gone two hours before Lazarus died. In that hot country a man has to be buried the same day. In Jerusalem I was shocked to find a man who died in the morning was buried in the afternoon. Sometimes a man would be apparently in good health in the morning, and that night he was in his grave.

Those two sisters closed their brother's eyes in death, and heard his last message – he might have left a message for Christ. They put the last kiss on his cheek, and then followed him to the sepulchre, and saw the stone rolled to the door. Then they went sorrowfully back to their desolate home. How they longed for Christ to come!

One day and night pass, and He does not come. The second and third day and night pass, and He does not come. When death enters a home, and some members of the family are at a distance, how we watch for the train to bring them back! How we long for their sympathy and comfort in that hour!

The fourth day came, and the messenger returned. How eagerly those sisters inquire if he had found Jesus!

"Yes, I found Him."

"Where?"

"Beyond Jordan, where John used to baptize."

"And did you tell Him that Lazarus was sick?"

"Yes, I told Him he was dangerously ill, that it was thought he wouldn't live."

"And what did He say?"

"He said the sickness wasn't unto death."

"Did He talk of coming?"

"He said, Yes, He would come."

"Did He come with you?"

"No, He went on preaching."

"Did He seem troubled?"

"No."

"Did He seem concerned?"

"No; He said the sickness wasn't unto death."

A strange look passed between those two sisters. Perhaps when they were alone Martha said to Mary:

"Can it be possible that we have been deceived in that preacher? If it had been Elijah or Elisha, he would have known that Lazarus was dead before the message got there; and yet He said the sickness wasn't unto death."

Still they watched and waited for Jesus to come. At night they listened for His footfall; but the fourth night rolled away, and the fifth morning dawned, and He had not come. How long the days were, how long the hours! It seemed as if the hours were as long as days. But, perhaps about four o'clock in the afternoon, as the sun was sinking behind those buildings in Jerusalem and throwing a shadow over the slope at Bethany, suddenly up out of the valley of the Jordan came Christ with His disciples. It may be that a little boy running into the house first told Martha, who was probably in the kitchen getting supper for the mourners who had come out from Jerusalem to weep with them, that Christ had come. She didn't wait to call Mary, but rushed out and said as she met Him:

"If Thou hadst been here my brother had not died."

"Yes, but thy brother shall rise again."

"I know he will rise at the resurrection of the just, for he was such a good brother."

"I am the resurrection and the life."

The Raising of Lazarus

Then I imagine Christ looking around a little disappointed, as He said to Martha:

"Where is Mary? Go and call her."

Back into the house she went, and said to Mary:

"The Master is come, and calleth for thee."

Mary rises up, and as she meets Jesus, she says the very thing that Martha said, those ten words:

"Lord, if Thou hadst been here, my brother had not died."

But she was weeping, and her tears seemed to touch the fountain of His own heart, and Jesus wept with her. Oh, how much comfort I get out of the fact that Christ can be touched with the feeling of our infirmity, and that Christ wept with those two sisters at Bethany!

When He asked where they had put the body, they showed Him the place, but with no thought that Lazarus was to rise. But He had power over death, and all He had to do was to speak, and His old friend Lazarus heard His voice and recognized it, and came up out of that sepulchre, and went back into his Bethany home. What a night that must have been! I have often tried to picture that home – Martha still serving, and Mary still listening – and oh, how she drank in the words that fell from His lips in that hour!

> How much comfort I get out of the fact that Christ can be touched with the feeling of our infirmity.

Comforting Christ

But now the scene changes. Christ had come to her in the time of trouble, to aid and to comfort. After that Mary came to Christ in the time of His trouble. Take that thought home. Did you ever think that you could comfort Christ? We are always looking to Christ to comfort us, but there is a sense, I believe, in which each of us can comfort Him, if we will. Mary may not have received into her soul the thought that Christ was going to rise from the dead, but she had at least believed His word that He was going to die. If she had thought He was going to rise, I believe she would have been at the grave early on the third morning. No Roman soldier, no power on earth could have kept that loving heart away from that sepulchre. But she believed He was going to die, and so she took an alabaster box of ointment and broke it over Him.

Two Gifts Which Jesus Could Not Give Away

Did you ever think that there were only two gifts that were given to the Son of God when He was on earth that He could not give away? In the seventh chapter of Luke, we read of a poor woman who came with an alabaster box and anointed Him with ointment, and here Mary also takes a box and breaks it and pours out the precious ointment upon Him.

The disciples were indignant and found fault. The best things I have ever done since I became a Christian, I have been blamed for. People have found fault with me, and even the religious papers attack me for the best things that I have ever done. When I am dead and gone, people will acknowledge it. Oh, it is so hard when you are working for Christ to have His disciples indignant with you, and say bitter things!

When Mary broke that box and anointed Jesus, there was great indignation among the disciples. Judas, that traitor, that was already planning to sell his Lord, was the most indignant of all. He was treasurer of the company. Mary thought he had great influence, and undoubtedly esteemed him more highly than herself. She thought she was the least of His disciples, but, thank God, love just overflowed, and she broke that box and anointed Him.

It was a great thing when Samuel anointed David, but no king ever had such a kingly anointing as when Mary anointed Christ with that ointment that was so sweet and so precious. One of the disciples figured up the price, and said that it was worth three hundred pence! A penny would hire a man all day, so that one pound of ointment had cost a year's work.

But Jesus estimated the worth differently. He rebuked the disciples, and said: "Why trouble ye the woman? for she hath wrought a good work upon me. . . . For in that she hath poured this ointment on my body, she did it for my burial. Verily I say unto you, Wheresoever this gospel shall be preached in the whole world, there shall also this that this woman hath done be told for a memorial."

Think of it! Wherever the gospel of the Son of God is to be preached in this wide world, that story is to be told!

There is nothing lost that we do for Christ.

Ante-Mortem Gifts

I can imagine that Mary thought that if she waited until Jesus was dead she might not have a chance to anoint His body, and so she came before His death to anoint Him.

There is a lesson there. How very kind and thoughtful we are to a family that has lost some member, and what kind words are said after the person is dead and gone! Would it not be better to say a few of those good things before they go? Wouldn't it be well to give some of your bouquets before a man dies, and not go and load down his coffin? He can't enjoy them then.

It was beautiful for Mary to come in that hour when Jesus was going into the terrible darkness, and the shadow of the cross was already upon His path, and anoint Him for His burial. John says: "Then took Mary a pound of ointment of spikenard, very costly, and anointed the feet of Jesus and wiped His feet with her hair, and the house was filled with the odor of the ointment."

"The house was filled." Not only the house, but Jerusalem; not only Jerusalem, but Judea; not only Judea, but all Palestine; not only all Palestine, but, thank God, the whole world has been filled with that odor, and it has lost none of its fragrance yet. I believe that the sweet scent ascends to heaven itself!

That was the best act that Mary ever did, and yet, if she had asked the twelve, every one would have said:

"No, it would be a waste. Take your money and give it to the poor."

Thank God, she forgot the poor for a while, she forgot His disciples, she forgot herself, and love just flowed out, and she lavished her best possession upon her Lord.

There is just one more passage that refers to this. It is in Mark: "She hath done what she could: she is come aforehand to anoint my body to the burying."

"She hath done what she could!" God does not ask any man or woman to do more than that, but if every man and every woman will do what they can, how much will be accomplished every day of our lives! An angel can do no more than that.

It is said of Mrs. Comstock, that godly missionary to India, that she brought her children down to the steamer to send them back to this country. She couldn't educate them in India, so they were all to leave her and come back to America. She had never been separated from them one night since they were born.

> "She hath done what she could!" God does not ask any man or woman to do more than that.

The captain of the boat came and said, "Mrs. Comstock, I am sorry to tell you, but we are going to take up the gang-plank now. You must go ashore."

She fell on her knees and cried out, "Lord Jesus, I do this for Thee."

They say the best of history has never been written. It never has. That would be too small a thing for historians to notice, but do you tell me it wasn't noticed in heaven? That mother was willing to give up her children and let them come back to this country, while she stayed there to work for Christ.

A Missionary's Son

A good many years ago I was stopping in a home in the West, and saw there a bright boy about thirteen years old. He didn't bear the name of the family he was living with, and yet was treated like one of the family. I asked the lady of the house who he was, and she said:

"He is the son of a missionary. His parents couldn't educate their children in India, so they came back here. But they had learned the language of India, and they did not feel that it was right for them to stay. Finally, the husband said, 'You stay here and educate the children, and I will go back.' The mother said, 'No. God has used me there with you, and we will go together.' 'But,' the father said, 'you can't give up those children. You never have been separated from them since they were born. You can't leave them in this country, and go back.' She said, 'I can do it for Christ, if He wants me to.'"

They made it a matter of prayer and put a notice in the papers that they were going to leave their children, and asking Christian people to take and educate them. This lady saw the notice, and wrote that she would take one child and bring it up for Christ's sake. She said:

"His mother came and stayed a week, and observed everything. She watched the order and discipline in my family, and after she was convinced that it was a safe place to leave her boy, she set the day to leave. My room was adjoining hers, and when the time came to start, I heard her pray, 'Lord Jesus, help me now. I need Thee. Help me to give up this dear boy without a tear, that I may leave him with a smile. The last time he sees me

I don't want him to see a tear in my eye. O God, help me, and give me strength.'"

Then she said that mother came down and took her boy to her bosom, hugged him and kissed him with a smile on her face – not a tear – and left.

She went to five homes in the same way. She then returned to India, but only lived a year, and then went to meet her Lord and Master.

Some years afterwards I was preaching in Hartford, and found a young man who was in the habit of picking up the rough boys of the streets and bringing them to my meetings. He would sit with them around him, and after the sermon would try to lead those boys to Christ. It pleased me very much, and I asked who he was. They told me his name, and said that he was in the theological seminary. I found that he was one of those five sons, and all of them expected to return to India to take up the work that their father and mother had left.

There is no account of that in history, but it is known up in heaven.

Mary In Heaven

I imagine that there was no small stir when Mary of Bethany entered heaven. She stands as high on the page of Christian history as any woman that ever lived; higher than Eve, or Sarah, the wife of Abraham, or Rebecca, or Rachel, or the whole lot of them. I can see her coming up to the throne, and Jesus rises and says:

"Father, this is Mary that anointed Me for My burial."

I believe she did her work as faithfully as Paul did.

When the books come to be opened, we will find some hidden one that we have never heard of has accomplished a greater work than many a man or woman whose name is known through the world.

Oh, that God would help us to forget ourselves and just work for Him directly! Never mind what people say. Never mind what the disciples say. They were indignant at Mary. Christ was pleased with her. Let us please Him.

Oh, I meet these Marys once in a while, and it is refreshing to my soul! There was one in Wellesley, some years ago. She was very anxious to graduate at Wellesley, but when her father died, she stepped right out and went to teaching school, and sent her two brothers to the academy and to college. She stayed out of Wellesley fifteen years until she landed those two boys in the pulpit, and then she went back and finished her course. All honor to a woman that will do that!

Mary's Epitaph

I imagine when Mary died, if God had sent an angel to write her epitaph, he couldn't have done better than to put over her grave what Christ said:

"She hath done what she could."

I would rather have that said over my grave, if it could honestly be said, than to have all the wealth of the Rothschilds. Christ raised a monument to her that is more lasting than the monuments raised to Caesar or Napoleon. Their monuments crumble away, but hers endures. Her name never appeared in print while she was on earth, but to-day it is famous in three hundred and fifty languages.

We may never be great; we may never be known outside our circle of friends; but we may, like Mary, do what we can. May God help each one of us to do what we can! Life will soon be over; it is short at the longest. Let us rise and follow in the footsteps of Mary of Bethany.

Chapter 7

A Need for Revival[1]

There is nothing I am more concerned about just now than that God should revive His church in America. I believe it is the only hope for our republic, for I don't believe that a republican form of government can last without righteousness. It seems to me that every patriot, every man who loves his country, ought to be anxious that the church of God should be quickened and revived.

Revivals Are Scriptural

I think you will find that revivals[2] or awakenings are perfectly scriptural. In all ages God has been quickening His people. I don't know that they had any before the flood; if they had, perhaps there wouldn't have been a

---

[1] Address delivered on Wednesday morning, August 2, 1899, at East Northfield, Mass.

[2] Perhaps "awakening" is a better word than "revival," but the term "revival" is better known. – D. L. M.

flood. But they didn't believe in it, and the flood was the result of their wickedness. But after the flood, in the days of Moses, there was a mighty awakening when he was sent down into Egypt to bring the children of Israel out of the house of bondage; and from Moses right on down, whenever Israel went back into idolatry, God raised up prophets and men of God to bring the nation back to Him. I used to think that I would like to have lived in the days of one of those prophets; but I have got over that, because the prophets appeared on the scene only when everything was dark as midnight, and Israel had fallen away from the worship of Jehovah to serve the gods of the nations around them. Then God used the prophets to call His people back.

It was dark when Samuel appeared. Eli's family had gone astray, the ark of God had fallen into the hands of the enemy, and everything was dark. But read those verses in I. Samuel 7:3, 4 –

> "And Samuel spake unto all the house of Israel, saying, If ye do return unto the Lord with all your hearts, then put away the strange gods and Ashtaroth from among you, and prepare your hearts unto the Lord, and serve Him only; and He will deliver you out of the hand of the Philistines. Then the children of Israel did put away Baalim and Ashtaroth, and served the Lord only."

Then in the eleventh verse we see the result, in that Israel smote their enemies. It has always been so in the history of man. Whenever man has repented and put away his idols and served God only, then God has come with mighty power and driven out the enemy.

In the days of Elijah midnight darkness had settled upon the land, and God used him to bring about a mighty revival. God raised up Jeremiah to draw the people back, and some heard his voice and took warning; but others persisted in living in their sins, saying, "We will not walk in the old ways." The result was that they went into captivity.

Enemies of God's Work

Every true work of God has had its bitter enemies – not only outside, but also inside – just as in the days of Nehemiah. There are usually some good people who join with the ungodly, and lift up their voice against the work of God. The best work usually meets the strongest opposition. A man may go into a town and preach for ten years with all the eloquence of Demosthenes, and draw great crowds, and if there are no conversions the papers will applaud him, and there will be a great many fine things said about him. But let there be a few hundred conversions, and the opposition will grow as hot as hell can make it. It always has been, and always will be. The nearer a man

> Whenever man has repented and served God only, then God has come with mighty power and driven out the enemy.

lives to Christ, and the more truth he has, the more bitter and vile will be the things that are said against him by the enemies of God.

Did this world ever have such a preacher as John the Baptist, except the Master Himself? See how bitter the opposition was, not only among bad people, but among the so-called good men of that time. His ministry was very short; but it was like a breath of spring after a long dark winter's night. Then came Christ with His apostles, and they did a great work, and yet met opposition everywhere.

Denominations Born in Revivals

Now, I cannot for the life of me see how any man or woman who knows the Bible can throw his influence against a revival. I am amazed to find, in the history of the church, denomination after denomination setting their faces against what I call the work of God.

The Roman Catholic church claims to be apostolic. How then can they be opposed to revivals, when the Christian church was born at Pentecost? That was the mightiest revival this world has ever seen, and yet the Catholic church does not like that word "revival," although the priests hold "missions," which are the same thing.

If the Episcopal church can trace their line back to Pentecost, they too are a child of a revival. I don't see how any Episcopalian can set his face against a revival. The older the church is the more it needs to be revived, because the tendency is into formalism.

Then where did the Lutheran church come from, if it wasn't born of a revival in the days of Martin Luther? How any Lutheran can set his face against revivals is a mystery to me. And God have mercy on a Methodist who doesn't believe in revivals, because that church sprang right straight out of a revival almost in our own day. Where did Methodism come from, if not from the revival under Charles and John Wesley and George Whitfield? Wasn't the nation stirred mightily under the preaching of these men? Where did the Quakers come from if not from a revival under Fox? Is not our Young Men's Christian Association a result of the revival of '57? All our best institutions have sprung out of revivals; and yet many people are afraid of them, and bring up objection after objection against them.

Some Objections to Revivals

One popular objection is: *So many converts do not hold out.*

That is quite true. If all the people who have professed conversion had been faithful, we would have had this world brought to Christ long before now. But you know, I find that some ministers, and elders, and deacons, do not hold out. If all held out, it would be contrary to scriptural experience. This argument against revivals does not bear looking into. The professed converts did not hold out in Christ's day. In John vi. we read:

> "Many of His disciples went back, and walked no more with Him."

Suppose that the farmer should refuse to sow because all his seed doesn't take root and ripen. Suppose that we should cut down our apple trees because all the blossoms don't mature. It is estimated that over ninety per cent of the men who go into business fail. Suppose that men would not enter business because so many business men fail. That is the argument that people bring against revivals: "They don't all hold out." A child is born, but I cannot rejoice, because so many children die. A man tumbles into the river, and another man jumps in and pulls him out. He wants me to rejoice, but I cannot, because I am afraid he may fall in again. That is the strongest argument that people bring against revivals.

Another argument which seems to have great weight with many people is: *There is so much excitement.*

My dear friends, I wish I could see as much excitement in the church of God, in the work of God, as I see in other things. If you want excitement, go to some place of amusement! I know of a minister who preached a very eloquent sermon against a revival meeting that Mr. Sankey and I were to hold in Great Britain. The whole argument of the sermon was against "undue excitement," and on Friday night he had been floor manager at a dance, and was there until five o'clock on Saturday morning. Then I suppose he wrote this eloquent sermon against "undue excitement in religious meetings"! Some saloons keep open all night, and men get so excited that they knock one another down, and kill one another, and yet we must not have revivals because there is "undue excitement." There is more excitement in the billiard halls and gambling dens, brothels and drinking saloons, in one week, than there is in the whole church of God in one year.

Newspapers can say nothing. If there is anybody under the sun that tries to get up sensations, it is the reporter. If there isn't any sensation in sight, he makes one. He is the last that should throw stones at us.

I am not so afraid of excitement as some people. The moment there comes a breath of interest, some people cry, "Sensationalism, sensationalism!" But, I tell you what, I would rather have sensation than stagnation any time. There is nothing a seaman fears so much as fog; he does not fear a storm nearly as much. We have too much fog in the church; let us get out of it. Get any preacher befogged, and he will say,

"I cannot draw the crowds, but then, thank God, I am no sensationalist!"

Let him write a book so dry that it will almost catch fire, and no one thinks of reading it. But he thanks God he is no sensationalist!

Do you think there was ever a country in the wide world stirred as Palestine was under the preaching of John the Baptist, and of Jesus and His apostles? Don't be afraid of a little excitement and a little "sensationalism." It seems to me that almost anything is preferable to deadness.

There is no excitement or sensationalism in a graveyard – a man lies where they put him; but I think there will be a stir on the resurrection morning. Where there is life, there will always be a commotion.

What we need is *life!* I don't believe that our young men would go off on bicycles every Sunday, or spend the day reading newspapers, if we had more life in the church.

A Scotch minister went to labor with one of his members who was in the habit of going to sleep during the sermon every Sunday.

"Don't you think," said he, "you had better stay at home if you can't keep awake?"

But she said that she was brought up to attend church, and she would go.

"Then don't you think you'd better take a little more snuff to keep you awake?"

She replied, "Don't you think you'd better put a little more snuff in your sermons, mon?"

People ought to get stirred up over eternal life and death.

An Experience in a Western Town

I stopped in a town of six thousand people out West last winter. A great many of the inhabitants were young men, some of them graduates of our colleges, who had gone out into that new country to make their way in the world. They were enterprising fellows.

They had four churches and thirty-six saloons in that town. Some of the saloons and concert halls were open day and night, summer and winter; but they closed up most of the churches in summer. The Episcopal minister's lungs had given out, and so he had gone off, and they couldn't have any preaching in the Episcopal church. The Baptist minister had died, so there was no preaching there. The Methodist minister had only one lung, and about all he could do was to whisper. There was one more minister, and when I got there he was preaching against revivals, warning his people not to be carried away by the meetings I was to hold.

I found that only two young men between the ages of fifteen and thirty belonged to those churches, and one of them only had one lung, and he was laid on his back at the first meeting, so I only had one young man left. One young man between fifteen and thirty in the church, and that minister preaching against revivals! I tell you it is enough to make the angels weep. Was anything under heaven needed more than a revival to save those young men, who had gone from some of the best homes in this country, and were spending their time and their money in those saloons and dens of iniquity? God have mercy on that minister!

A bishop once said to me: "We don't believe in revivals. We believe in taking them in childhood, like Timothy, and training them up in the church."

But didn't Paul say Timothy was begotten by him? I have an idea that Timothy was converted in one of Paul's meetings.

A minister said to me in one place: "I hope this work will turn out better than the last we had here. I took one hundred into my church, and can only find two of them now."

It was very depressing. I said to another minister in the same city:

"If I thought this work wasn't going to turn out any better than that, I would rather go to sweeping the streets or breaking stones."

"Why," said he, "I took in about one hundred at that time, and I can put my hand on all but three. One moved out of the city, and two fell away, but ninety-seven out of the hundred are doing well."

That was five or six years after the revival.

If that first minister had been honest he would have told me that the moment his church got those young converts in, they thought it was a good time to move out of a poor neighborhood into the aristocratic part of the city. The church split, and he not only lost the young converts, but the old ones, too, and the church went to pieces.

> If there are counterfeit revivals we are not going to give up the real ones.

I believe that if we ask God for a real work, He won't give us a counterfeit. If we ask God for bread, He isn't going to give us a stone. If we have counterfeit dollars there must be genuine dollars somewhere; and if there are counterfeit revivals – and the devil tries to counterfeit everything – we are not going to give up the real ones. People stretch their necks and say, "Where are the people converted in that great revival?" I don't know; but I do know that they are not going to go around to your house and ring the front door bell, and tell you where they are. If you set your face against revivals, you are the last person they will come to.

The Skeptic and the Missionary

Some men in London, who had returned from India, gave a dinner party. Among others who were invited were a wealthy merchant, who was a skeptic, and a foreign missionary. During the dinner party they brought up the question of native converts, and the English merchant turned up his nose, and said:

"I have lived in India for twenty years, but I have heard more about native converts in London than I ever heard in India. I never saw one native convert all the years I was there."

The guests looked for a reply from the foreign missionary, but he said nothing until later in the evening, when he turned to this man and said:

"Did you ever see any tigers in India?"

The merchant's face lit up at once.

"Oh, yes," he said, "I have not only seen them, but I have shot a good many."

"That is strange," said the missionary, "I have been in India for twenty years, and I have never seen a tiger."

One had been looking for tigers and the other for converts. You generally get what you look for.

I was on the Pacific coast for six months, and I didn't go to a place where I didn't meet people who had been converted in Boston, in the Hippodrome in New York, and in Agricultural Hall or Haymarket Theatre or Campbell Hall in London. Everywhere I found ministers, deacons, elders, or Sabbath-school workers, who had been converted in places where I had been.

I could doubt my existence as easily as I could doubt that God not only converts, but keeps.

Some people have an idea that where a great number are brought out at one time they are not so healthy. I don't believe a word of it. If one or two come into the church the minister never thinks of preparing a whole sermon for them. But let him take in one hundred young converts, and he will get up sermon after sermon to build up those young converts in the faith. Not only that, but it will make such a stir that every member of the church will be interested in helping them.

Our Need of a Revival

I come to another point, and that is *our need*.

When God has revived His work there has always been great need; it is darkest just before the dawn. I think it is getting very dark, but don't think for a moment that I am a pessimist. If I should live ten thousand years I couldn't be a pessimist. I haven't any more doubt about the final outcome of things than I have of my existence. I believe Jesus is going to sway His sceptre to the ends of the earth, that the time is coming when God's will is to be done on earth as it is done in heaven, and when man's voice will be only the echo of God's. I believe the time is coming when every knee will bow and every tongue confess Christ.

I am no pessimist, and I am not under the juniper tree, either. If I look on the dark side it is to stir you up and get you to fighting. But it is getting dark; there is no doubt about that. Paul says in his second letter to Timothy:

"This know also, that in the last days perilous times shall come. For men shall be lovers of their own selves."

Is not that true to-day? Lovers of their own selves. Deny it if you can. Look at the men who are selfishly piling up their millions. I am a young man yet, and I can remember when we had hardly a millionaire in this country. When a man got his million he had enough. But now, two, three or five hundred millions don't satisfy.

"Covetous, boasters, proud, blasphemers, disobedient to parents, unthankful, unholy." Now listen. "Without natural affection, truce-breakers, false accusers, incontinent, fierce, despisers of those that are good."

For a year that saying has been ringing through the nation, "Remember the Maine." Less than three hundred men lost their lives on the Maine, but every twenty-four hours three hundred men go down to drunkards' graves in this country. "Void of natural affection." I would rather have a son kill me outright than take five years to kill me by drinking. That is what is going on in this country all the time. Instead of crying, "Remember the Maine," I think you would better cry, "Remember whiskey," and rise up and put down the devilish traffic. In four years there were 38,512 murders in the United States, and in the same length of time England had less than 600. Lynching is unknown in the old country, and we are having lynchings by the scores and hundreds. Last year we had 25,000 divorces. See how Sabbath-breaking is increasing, and dishonesty in business. Look at the bank presidents and cashiers who are in our jails and prisons. Do we not need a reformation? Hasn't the time come for the children of God to cry out, O God, revive Thy work!

"Traitors, heady, high-minded, lovers of pleasures more than lovers of God." I was bearing down on the bicycle here to the students a few weeks ago, setting forth that one of the great temptations they were going to have was the bicycle. There is no doubt it is a blessing; but all these blessings may become a curse if you don't look out. I told the students they would be tempted to take their bicycles and go out into the country and neglect their souls, neglect the church of God, neglect Sabbath-schools, neglect Bible classes. One of my Christian friends thought I was making a mistake, but he has been away the last few weeks, and he said to me last night:

"I want to tell you I made a mistake. I have seen something that has made my heart ache."

I don't believe any one can see the vast throng of young men in our cities – and I am sorry to say, bad women, too – on their bicycles going off into the country and fields and woods to spend the Sabbath, and trampling the law of God into the dust, filling their pockets with Sunday newspapers – and these are their bibles – it wouldn't have been tolerated a few years ago! It wouldn't have been countenanced in Chicago a few years ago that they should have their theaters open Sunday afternoon and night, but that is the case. A bill went into the New York Legislature recently to allow the theaters to open on Sunday in New York City; and I said to one of the prominent politicians:

"I hope you will put your heel on that bill, and do all you can to kill it."

"No," he said, "I believe in it. That is what we want. I go to mass Sunday morning, but I think our Lord meant us to have the rest of the day for recreation."

Serving the God of the Hebrews in the morning, and Baal in the afternoon and evening! The curse of the age is people want two altars, one for Baal and one for Jehovah. You cannot do it; there must be separation! We need a revival to clear the air.

The Gospel and Its Counterfeits

Another idea that is very prevalent, is that people will not hear the old gospel, and that *the old gospel has lost some of its power.*

I don't believe one word of it. There is a lot of stuff that men call the gospel that has no more gospel in it than there is wheat in sawdust; but some people don't seem to know the difference. I heard some time ago of a young wife who had a certain amount given her every week, from which she was to pay all the household bills and keep an account. After a few months the husband said:

"Darling, I will stay at home this evening, and we will look over the accounts and see how we are getting along."

They looked them over carefully, and he saw that

every week she had balanced her accounts by charging something to "G. K. W."

The husband began to wonder who this man was, and asked:

"Who is this G. K. W.?"

She explained that she could never balance the account, so she always put something down to "Goodness knows what."

When we hear some people preach, we have to put it down, "G. K. W. – goodness knows what."

I honestly say that I have heard some able men preach, and I didn't know what they were talking about. I suppose I am about the average; and if I couldn't understand, what about the rest? I want to say, if you put the old gospel straight and square, it has as much effect as it ever had.

It is a false idea that people want a new kind of gospel, and that the preaching has lost its power. Man is the same as he has been for six thousand years. Sin leaped into the world full grown. The first born of woman was a murderer. We are a bad lot; and what you want is to tell men so – not flatter them, and tell them how angelic they are because they have some education. An educated rascal is the meanest kind of a rascal.

A Fair Test

Last winter, when I was out on the Pacific coast, I read in a paper that a minister said my preaching no longer had the same effect it used to. I said to myself, Is that so? I began to wake up, and said, Well, now, I will take note.

The next Sunday I was preaching in the Mormon tabernacle in Salt Lake City; there were probably seven thousand people there. I commenced on sin. I believe Mormons are just as much sinners as the rest of us. I bore down as hard as I could on sin; and when I got through, I said:

"You have heard this. Do you want to break with sin? Are you tired and sick of sin?" I said, "Take time to consider; don't act on the impulse, but just consider. *If* there is one in this house that wants to break with sin, I am going to ask you to rise and stand while I pray."

I put it fair and square, and gave them perhaps five minutes before I brought them to a decision, and do you know, almost the whole crowd rose! Tears rolled down their cheeks.

Now, I preached a few years ago in Salt Lake City, and I didn't get the result I did right then and there.

The next Sunday I was preaching in Detroit, and I had a meeting for men in one of the largest churches there Sunday afternoon. I preached on the same subject – sin – and when I got through, I said:

"You know whether you want to break with sin or not. Now face the issue." I took some time just to explain so they wouldn't act just because others did. "Now," I said, "I don't want a man in this house to get up because someone else does. If you want to break with sin, I am going to ask you to rise while I pray for you."

That audience of two thousand young men, cashiers of banks, clerks, merchants, rose in a mass. I preached in Detroit years ago, and I never got such a result as that. It was the first Sunday I was there, and the first time I ever met that audience, too; but they were like clay in the hands of the potter.

I thought I would make this a little more personal, so I said, "If you men after prayer really mean this, stay and let us talk with you." Over two hundred young men stayed; they were tired and sick of sin.

The next Sunday I was preaching at Yale. You can't tell much about the first service in the college chapel, because the students are obliged to attend, whether they want to or not. I took the same subject, sin. I didn't spare them. In the evening it was optional with them whether they came or not, but we had a hall crowded, and when I put the question I found there were more inquirers in Yale than I had ever seen. I have been going there for twenty years, and I have never had such results as I had right then and there.

The fourth Sunday I preached in the Maryland penitentiary. There is a new kind of audience: Mormons, merchants and clerks, students in Yale, and then penitentiary men.

Now I was in Baltimore for six months in 1878-9, and preached every Sunday morning in the penitentiary. When I preached there twenty years ago, I preached four or five Sundays before I dared to ask for any expression, but last Spring when I got through preaching the same sermon against sin, all over that audience men were weeping and asking to be prayed for.

Four Sundays, four different kinds of people, but the same results throughout! Don't tell me that the gospel hasn't the same power it had of old! Don't tell me that men need any different kind of preaching. What we should do is to cry down sin and lift up Jesus Christ, God's remedy for sin. There is as much power to-day to save men as there ever has been, and men are the same – human nature hasn't changed one whit – and the quicker we find that out, the better.

I believe that you can go into almost any audience in America, and ask those that have been converted in the time of a revival to rise, and four-fifths of the church members will stand up. I have tried it over and over again all over this country, and I have yet to find one place where it wasn't so.

A Hush from Heaven

Another thing that encourages me to believe that there are hopeful signs is that there has come a hush on the meetings during the last six months that I haven't seen for a number of years.

I preached last Sunday in Dr. Storrs' church, in Brooklyn. I have been going to Brooklyn and New York for twenty or thirty years; Mr. Sankey has been with me at different meetings. I venture to say he cannot get up and contradict this statement, that there was a hush in that meeting, and a power, that we have seldom had for twenty or thirty years, from the time it began until we got through. It was a hot day in July, when people think nothing can be done, but that audience was just as if it was held by some unseen power, and it seemed as if God Almighty was speaking to the people.

God is coming very near us. I believe we are on the eve of a mighty work if we will just rise and claim it.

The Demand for Bibles and Bible Teaching

And another hopeful sign is that there has never been such a demand for Bibles in the history of this world as there has been during the last few years; never. One of the New York editors said to me when I was in New York some time ago,

"Mr. Moody, is there any demand for Bibles now?"

I said, "Any demand for Bibles! Man, where did you come from? Why, there has never been such a demand for Bibles in the history of the world as there is at present."

He replied, laughingly, "If you had said that to me a few months ago, I never would have believed it; but the question came up in our office that the Bible was becoming a back number and the Sunday newspaper taking its place, and we were going to write up an editorial. I sent out to some of the book-stores to see if there was any demand for Bibles, and to my great amazement they reported that there never had been such a demand for Bibles as there had been in the last three years. I couldn't understand it."

"Where did you go?" I asked.

He sent to a few of the stores and the Bible Societies.

I said, "You didn't go quite far enough. If you had

gone to some of these department stores, you would have found they sell Bibles by the ton." There is one department store in Philadelphia that has sold more books than ten of the leading publishing houses. They take a Bible like this that I have always paid seven or eight dollars for – not quite so good paper, and not quite so well bound, but same size and same type – and they sell it for seventy cents; think of it! There never has been such competition in selling the Word of God.

It is said, of Martin Luther's day, that his books and pamphlets and the truth of his preaching dropped down on the nations, and were scattered by the angels. It seems as if the angels of God were just moving in a marvelous way, and people were going back to the old Book.

I used to say to the superintendent of our Bible Institute in Chicago that I wished we could have classes in the evening. We have had now for ten years a Bible lecture at nine o'clock in the morning and another at eleven o'clock, right in the heart of Chicago. I wanted to have classes in the evening.

"Well," he said, "the churches work their members pretty well. They have the Epworth League, and the Young People's meetings, and the Christian Endeavor; they have the Young Men's Christian Association, and weekly prayer-meetings. I don't know that we can make it work, but we will try it."

And so two years ago last winter we had one evening lecture, and the average attendance right through the course was five hundred, and there was no attraction that came to Chicago that could draw those people away. It was so successful that some city ministers said, "Can't we have classes in our churches?" Nothing suited me any better, and so next winter similar lectures were given in five sections in Chicago, and the average attendance for the whole season was twenty-seven hundred. Last winter the demand was stronger than ever, and the average attendance from October to May was about six thousand people, meeting every week to study the Word of God.

I believe when God revives His work, people will go back to His Book. People are tired and sick of this awful controversy. Sam Jones' motto has been, "Quit your meanness." I hope the motto of the ministers of this country will be, "Quit your fighting and go to work, and preach the simple gospel."

Now the question is, shall we have a great and mighty harvest, or shall we go on discussing our differences? As far as I am concerned, I am terribly tired of it, and I would like before I go hence to see the whole church of God quickened as it was in '57, and a wave going from Maine to California that shall sweep thousands into the kingdom of God.

Why not?

Talk about this work not lasting; Pentecost isn't over yet! The revival of '57 isn't over yet by a good deal. Some of the best men we have in our churches were brought out in '57. Why shouldn't we have now at the close of this old century a great shaking up and a mighty wave from heaven? Are you doing anything to hinder it?

Dwight L. Moody
– A Brief Biography

Dwight Lyman Moody was born on February 5, 1837, in Northfield, Massachusetts. His father died when Dwight was only four years old, leaving his mother with nine children to care for. When Dwight was seventeen years old, he left for Boston to work as a salesman. A year later, he was led to Jesus Christ by Edward Kimball, Moody's Sunday school teacher. Moody soon left for Chicago and began teaching a Sunday school class of his own. By the time he was twenty-three, he had become a successful shoe salesman, earning $5,000 in only eight months, which was a lot of money for the middle of the nineteenth century. Having decided to follow Jesus, though, he left his career to engage in Christian work for only $300 a year.

D. L. Moody was not an ordained minister, but was an effective evangelist. He was once told by Henry Varley, a British evangelist, "Moody, the world has yet to see what God will do with a man fully consecrated to Him."

Moody later said, "By God's help, I aim to be that man."

It is estimated that during his lifetime, without the help of television or radio, Moody traveled more than one million miles, preached to more than one million people, and personally dealt with over seven hundred and fifty thousand individuals.

D. L. Moody died on December 22, 1899.

Moody once said, "Some day you will read in the papers that D. L. Moody, of East Northfield, is dead. Don't you believe a word of it! At that moment I shall be more alive than I am now. I shall have gone up higher, that is all – out of this old clay tenement into a house that is immortal; a body that death cannot touch, that sin cannot taint, a body fashioned like unto His glorious body. I was born of the flesh in 1837. I was born of the Spirit in 1856. That which is born of the flesh may die. That which is born of the Spirit will live forever."

Other Similar Titles

The Overcoming Life, by Dwight L. Moody

Are you an overcomer? Or, are you plagued by little sins that easily beset you? Even worse, are you failing in your Christian walk, but refuse to admit and address it? No Christian can afford to dismiss the call to be an overcomer. The earthly cost is minor; the eternal reward is beyond measure.

Dwight L. Moody is a master at unearthing what ails us. He uses stories and humor to bring to light the essential principles of successful Christian living. Each aspect of overcoming is looked at from a practical and understandable angle. The solution Moody presents for our problems is not religion, rules, or other outward corrections. Instead, he takes us to the heart of the matter and prescribes biblical, God-given remedies for every Christian's life. Get ready to embrace genuine victory for today, and joy for eternity.

Available where books are sold.

The Way to God, by Dwight L. Moody

There is life in Christ. Rich, joyous, wonderful life. It is true that the Lord disciplines those whom He loves and that we are often tempted by the world and our enemy, the devil. But if we know how to go beyond that temptation to cling to the cross of Jesus Christ and keep our eyes on our Lord, our reward both here on earth and in heaven will be 100 times better than what this world has to offer.

This book is thorough. It brings to life the love of God, examines the state of the unsaved individual's soul, and analyzes what took place on the cross for our sins. *The Way to God* takes an honest look at our need to repent and follow Jesus, and gives hope for unending, joyous eternity in heaven.

Available where books are sold.

How to Study the Bible,
by Dwight L. Moody

There is no situation in life for which you cannot find some word of consolation in Scripture. If you are in affliction, if you are in adversity and trial, there is a promise for you. In joy and sorrow, in health and in sickness, in poverty and in riches, in every condition of life, God has a promise stored up in His Word for you.

This classic book by Dwight L. Moody brings to light the necessity of studying the Scriptures, presents methods which help stimulate excitement for the Scriptures, and offers tools to help you comprehend the difficult passages in the Scriptures. To live a victorious Christian life, you must read and understand what God is saying to you. Moody is a master of using stories to illustrate what he is saying, and you will be both inspired and convicted to pursue truth from the pages of God's Word.

Available where books are sold.

Daniel, Man of God,
by Dwight L. Moody

God will exalt us when the time is right. We needn't try to promote ourselves; we needn't struggle for position. Let God put us where He wants us and let us be true to God. It is better for a man to be right with God, even if he holds no great earthly position. It is honest and humble men whom God will promote, if He so desires.

This study illustrates what Daniel did, and also what Daniel didn't do, which caught the attention of God and kings alike. Few are the men in history of Daniel's caliber, even though the principles he followed can be implemented by all. Are you ready to be a truly great man, one that will cause God and men to take notice?

Available where books are sold.

www.ingramcontent.com/pod-product-compliance
Lightning Source LLC
Chambersburg PA
CBHW070145080526
44586CB00015B/1850